THE GOVERNMENT AND
POLITICS OF
COMMUNIST CHINA

DEREK J. WALLER received his Ph.D. from the University of London, and is currently assistant professor of Political Science at Vanderbilt University in Nashville, Tennessee. He was educated at the London School of Economics and the London School of Oriental and African Studies, and attended the Universities of Indiana and Stanford. He is the author of *Politics and the Kiangsi Soviet* (forthcoming), *Comparative Communist Political Leadership* (forthcoming, with Carl Beck *et al.*), and a recent monograph, *Stasis and Change in Revolutionary Elites: A Comparative Analysis of the 1956 Party Central Committees in China and the USSR* (with Robert H. Donaldson). Professor Waller has also been a contributor to various professional journals.

THE GOVERNMENT AND POLITICS OF COMMUNIST CHINA

Derek J. Waller

ANCHOR BOOKS

Doubleday & Company, Inc.
Garden City, New York
1971

The Government and Politics of Communist China was originally published by Hutchinson University Library in 1970. The Anchor Books edition is published by arrangement with Hutchinson University Library.

Anchor Books edition: 1971

To my parents

CONTENTS

People's Liberation Army, Air force, Navy — Functions
of the armed forces — Command structure and political
control — The armed forces and the Cultural
Revolution — Nuclear weapons development — The
militia

ACKNOWLEDGMENTS

My thanks go to Professor William A. Robson, the general editor of the Politics series for Hutchinson University Library, for constructive criticism and advice given at all stages of preparation of this book. I am also very much indebted to Dr Davis B. Bobrow, Dr Robert H. Donaldson, Dr Audrey Donnithorne, Dr Paul H. B. Godwin, Dr Ian Mabbett and Mr Daniel Tretiak, all of whom read portions of the manuscript and offered valuable comments. Naturally, I remain responsible for any errors. For typing services rendered with alacrity, I should like to thank Mrs Lane Byrd, Mrs Jacqueline Greer and Miss Elizabeth McKee.

D.J.W.

4

ACKNOWLEDGMENTS

I, thanks are to Bernard Wheel...e...band the ...of the Public Health Foundation Chicago Library ...the ....collecting...help...of...of...the...experience of this book. I ....o...I also to Dr. Elisabeth Burrow, Dr. John O. ...., V. Pierre Desmarais, E...M. H.R. Sutton, Dr. Ro. Mercier, Dr. Paul L. Ross...l...or V. ...and...partners or...have ...so offer...valuable comments. ...I... much regret how I still have ...comments. For those errors as remained still all only, and that ...I may not I ...ur, which ...and ...f...have only and ...which...m...enoch, know...

ABBREVIATIONS

APC	Agricultural Producers' Cooperative
AR	Autonomous Region
CC	Central Committee
CCP	Chinese Communist Party
Comintern	Communist International
CPGC	Central People's Government Council
CPPCC	Chinese People's Political Consultative Conference
ECCI	Executive Committee of the Communist International
GAC	Government Administration Council
Hsiang	A group of villages
KMT	Kuomintang, or Nationalist Party
MAC	Military Affairs Committee
NPC	National People's Congress
PLA	People's Liberation Army
Politburo	Political Bureau
PRC	People's Republic of China
SEATO	South East Asia Treaty Organisation
USSR	Union of Soviet Socialist Republics
YCL	Young Communist League

1

THE CHINESE REVOLUTION

The impact of the West

For thousands of years the Chinese considered themselves to be at the centre of the world, and indeed their name for their own country was "Middle Kingdom", which symbolised the central position of Chinese civilisation, surrounded by an abundance of lesser cultures. The latter, which were either ruled directly from Peking or acknowledged the authority of Peking, included both Inner and Outer Mongolia, Tibet, Sinkiang, Burma, Korea and Vietnam. The influence of Peking over these dependent countries varied directly with the political and military strength of the Chinese government. Relations between Peking and its vassal states were regulated by the "tribute system", whereby the barbarian chiefs sent gifts, or tribute, to the Chinese Emperor, thereby acknowledging his suzerainty over them.

Over the centuries, the tribute system served as a cloak for trading relations between the Chinese and the surrounding areas. From the early sixteenth century this system, regulating as it did relations between superiors and inferiors, was increasingly disrupted by the sea-borne traders of expansionist European states. First the Portuguese and Spanish, and then the Dutch and British in the seventeenth century, were all treated like any other tribute-bearing nations. Trade was carried on through official Chinese government monopolies at Macao and Canton on the south-east coastline, remote from Peking. Increasingly, the West and in particular the British, whose East India Company was doing a thriving business exporting opium to China, protested against restrictions on the freedom of trade, requested the opening of more ports, and demanded diplomatic equality between the two countries. Missions sent from England failed to obtain these concessions, and they were only granted by the first of the "unequal treaties" forced upon China at Nanking in 1842 after her defeat in the Opium War. This treaty also saw the start of "extra-territoriality" whereby Europeans in the treaty-ports were subject not to Chinese, but to Western law.

In addition to external defeat, China was also suffering from internal problems. Agriculture was the major economic activity, and as opportunities for upward mobility belonged mainly to the landlord-gentry class, over the centuries the ownership of land had become concentrated in very few hands. The mass of the peasantry however, living at subsistence levels, was quickly reduced to starvation by natural disasters such as floods or drought. Tremendous increases in population (from 60 million in 1500 to 430 million in 1850), due largely to new imported crops such as the sweet potato, were not coupled with corresponding increases in arable land. In addition, the drain on silver, needed to pay for opium imports, raised its value, and therefore raised taxes, which were based on silver. These economic causes were linked to political factors, in particular Chinese dislike of the reigning Manchu dynasty, and the corruption and weakness of the military revealed in the war against the British. A combination of these factors, combined with widespread floods and famine, produced the peasant Taiping Rebellion of the mid-nineteenth century.

The Taiping Rebellion was not the first or the last peasant rebellion of the century, but it differed from the others not only because it was the most devastating, killing at least twenty million people before it was finally suppressed after more than fifteen years, but also because it sought not just to replace the old dynasty with a new one, but to revolutionise Chinese society by abolishing the landlord and scholar-gentry classes.

The Taipings were eventually defeated with the assistance of the Western powers, who sought peace and stability in order to expand their commercial activities. These had improved considerably after their victory over China in the second Opium War of 1858–60, which had resulted in the invasion of Peking by an Anglo-French army, and had forced China to agree to, among other things, the opening up of yet more ports for trade and the granting of rights of diplomatic residence in Peking.

The continuing defeats by the European "barbarians",

coupled with domestic uprisings, forced the Emperor's Regent, the Empress Dowager, to embark on a programme of modernisation in the 1860s. Although this did produce some tangible results, in the shape of a Ministry of Foreign Affairs, and the building of a shipyard and arsenals, little real progress was made, because modernisation was always seen as the grafting of Western technology and institutions on to the Chinese value system. It was not until the twentieth century that it was realised that foreign technology and institutions were the products of a foreign social and political system and could not easily be transplanted into alien soil.

Under further encroachments from the West, and after a humiliating defeat by Japan in 1895, another reform programme was launched, this time by the Emperor Kuang-hsü in 1898. The reforms hurt the interests of the reactionaries, who staged a successful *coup d'état* under the leadership of the Empress Dowager. Faced by the failure of reform, radical Chinese turned to revolution. Loss of control by the dynasty was epitomised by the growth of the Boxers, a fanatically xenophobic sect active in north China, who besieged the foreign legations in Peking for two months in the summer of 1900, before the siege was lifted by a military expedition.

The Republican revolution

Sun Yat-sen, a Chinese who had been mainly educated abroad, drew on the support of the radical Chinese and Japanese intelligentsia, and the wealth of the overseas Chinese, to develop his struggle to overthrow the decaying Manchu dynasty, and replace it with a constitutional government. In 1905 he founded his Tung-meng Hui (Sworn Together Society), based on the three principles of nationalism, democracy and the people's livelihood, the last-named principle being a rather vague concept drawn from the ideas of Henry George, and favouring restrictions on private landlords.

After many unsuccessful attempts, a local uprising on 10 October 1911 triggered off the revolution. The Manchu dynasty, already in an advanced stage of decay, quickly crumbled, after having requested support from army strongman Yüan Shih-k'ai, who instead sided with the rebels. Sun Yat-sen, in the USA at the time, immediately returned to

i

China and was proclaimed as provisional President of the Chinese Republic on 1 January 1912. Military power, however, remained in the hands of Yüan Shih-k'ai, and when, in February, the Emperor P'u-yi (a child aged five) abdicated, Sun stepped down in favour of Yüan, who was favoured by the foreign powers as the only person capable of bringing peace and stability to China. Yüan's government was virtually without funds, and in order to cut down on domestic demands he granted semi-autonomy to provincial military leaders by allowing them to raise their own revenue, thus further weakening the central government and laying the basis for future warlord regimes based on regional power groups. Yüan then ignored and finally dissolved the cabinet and parliament set up by the Republic, and increasingly occupied himself with dreams of establishing a new dynasty. In 1915, he attempted to make himself Emperor, but failed, and died in 1916. China then entered more than a decade of warlordism.

The 1911 revolution had failed primarily because the revolutionaries had little in common beyond overthrowing the Manchu dynasty, and because there was little Chinese nationalism at that time to give support to the new Republic. In addition, such Western institutions as a cabinet and parliament did not flourish in China.

Warlordism

Warlordism meant that China fragmented into a number of conflicting regional units, each based on a locally recruited army, and often backed by one or other of the Great Powers seeking to defend their own interests. In the north, centred on Peking, the Anhwei group, backed by Chang Tso-lin of Manchuria, and by Japan, warred with the pro-British Chihli grouping of Wu P'ei-fu. In 1917 Peking was taken by the Chihli group, now supported by Chang Tso-lin, but disagreement between the two allies eventually led to fighting and the withdrawal of Chang to Manchuria in 1922. In the south of China there were other warlord groupings, and also Sun Yat sen's Kuomintang (or Nationalist Party) based in Canton (after 1917) where they cooperated with the local warlord and still claimed to be the true national government. The

Great Powers, however, turned a deaf ear to Sun, and tended to recognise as the government of China whichever faction was in control of Peking at the time.

May Fourth movement

With China enfeebled by internal conflict, and the attention of Europe fixed on the First World War, Japan saw her opportunity to benefit at China's expense. She declared war on Germany in 1914 and promptly seized the German concessions in Shantung. The following year Japan submitted to China the Twenty-One Demands, bidding China to cede the former German rights to Japan, and dictating other demands which would virtually have reduced China to a Japanese colony.

The Twenty-One Demands produced a wave of resentment and a boycott of Japanese goods. But after a show of force by Japan, Yüan Shih-k'ai was forced to accept many of the demands.

In 1917 China herself declared war on Germany, in response to pressure from the United States, and also in order to be included at the subsequent peace conference, and thus be able to demand her rights against those of Japan. Secretly, however, Japan had already entered into negotiations with Britain, France, and Russia to be allowed to keep the German concessions after the war. Consequently, China's request, at the Versailles Peace Conference of January 1919, for a return to her of the German bases in Shantung, was refused. In the larger urban areas of China there was a new sense of nationalism, stimulated in part by the publication of literature in the vernacular rather than the difficult classical style. Consequently an attentive public was following international events and was enraged by the Versailles decision. On May 4 the bitterness that had accumulated since the Twenty-One Demands exploded into a huge student demonstration in Peking, in which ministers who were pro-Japanese were manhandled. Further demonstrations followed throughout the country, accompanied by strikes and another boycott of Japanese products. Eventually, the government gave in, with the Chinese delegates to the Peace Conference refusing to sign the Peace Treaty, and leaving Versailles in June. The issue of the German rights in Shantung was only settled in 1922 with their return to China by Japan.

Birth of the Chinese Communist Party

The effect of the 4 May movement on the Chinese intellectuals, accompanied as it naturally was by a disillusionment with the West for having sold out China's rights to Japan, was coterminous with more favourable overtures from the new Bolshevik government in Russia, who had made a good impression by voluntarily renouncing such Tsarist privileges as extra-territoriality.

The initial effects of the 1917 October Revolution had been slight. Petrograd and Moscow were a long way off, and less distant Russian territories were still in the hands of the White armies. Nevertheless, Chinese translations of some of the essential writings of Marx and Lenin were gradually introduced into China, and a Marxist Study Group was established in Peking in 1918 by Li Ta-chao and Ch'en Tu-hsiu, teachers at Peking University. Several students joined, including the youthful Mao Tse-tung. The members of the study group propounded many different ideologies at that time, and looked at Marxism more from the standpoint of academic interest, rather than as true believers. However, under the influence of the events of 4 May 1919, and on becoming acquainted with more of the Marxist–Leninist texts, particularly Lenin's theory of imperialism, both Li and Ch'en were convinced Marxists by 1920.

Small groups of Marxists were therefore already in existence in China when the first emissary of the Communist International (founded by the Bolsheviks in 1919 to coordinate the activities of foreign communist parties) arrived in early 1920. This emissary, Voitinsky, met both Li Ta-chao and Ch'en Tu-hsiu, and held meetings of Marxist groups during the year, which formally coalesced into the Chinese Communist Party (CCP) when twelve delegates representing fifty members held the First Congress in Shanghai on 1 July 1921. Ch'en, although absent from the Congress, was elected General Secretary.

The programme of the CCP was an extreme "leftist" one—based on the proletariat, the Party would work for the victory of socialism in China, bypassing the capitalist stage, and without collaboration with the bourgeois-democrats. However, this was at variance with the views of Lenin, as set out in his "Theses on the National and Colonial Questions" at the Second Congress of the Comintern (Communist International) of 1920. Lenin, noting the almost total lack of an urban proletariat in most of the colonial and backward countries of the world, favoured local communist parties making temporary alliances with bourgeois-democratic movements in these countries, so as to advance their own influence and base of mass support, while retaining organisational independence, and awaiting the growth of an industrial labour force.

Lenin's proposals were accepted by the Chinese Communist Party at their Second Congress in July 1922, and it was decided to work for a two-party alliance with Sun Yat-sen's Kuomintang. Moscow had chosen the Kuomintang as the bourgeois-democratic party for the communists to ally with only after rejecting Wu P'ei-fu in Peking, following talks between Wu and Maring, a Comintern representative. The Comintern estimated that the Kuomintang had a better mass basis than the northern warlord, and a better revolutionary leader in Sun Yat-sen.

The alliance was not quickly arrived at. Sun initially rejected the offer of a two-party alliance, but said that he would not object to individual communists joining his party. This approach of the "bloc within", whereby individual communists would work inside the Kuomintang while the Communist Party would retain its external independence, was adopted as policy by the CCP in August 1922.

The motives of the Comintern were clear—they saw in the Kuomintang the best vehicle for the furtherance of Russian interests, and believed that the CCP would eventually be able to take control of the Kuomintang. Sun Yat-sen, on his side, was disillusioned with the West's treatment of China, and its non-recognition of his government. He also wanted the material aid of Russia in the form of arms and money, so as to build a strong army with which he could reunify China. Furthermore, he anticipated that he could keep the communists as an inferior partner within his organisation.

Throughout 1923 talks went on between Sun and the

Comintern representative Adolf Joffe, during which Sun agreed to have the Kuomintang reorganised on Bolshevik lines. In October 1923 the Comintern adviser Mikhail Borodin arrived in Canton to begin the transformation of the Kuomintang on a democratic-centralist basis, together with other Russian advisers to reorganise the Kuomintang army.

The alliance between the two parties, which had been formally accepted by the CCP at its Third Congress in June 1923, was concluded at the First Kuomintang Congress of January 1924. Three communists were elected to the Kuomintang's Central Executive Committee, and Mao Tse-tung was made an alternate member.

The First United Front 1924–7

Certain elements of friction between the two parties in the alliance had always been in existence, but it was only after the death of Sun Yat-sen in Peking in March 1925 that they began to come out into the open. In November 1925 a group of conservative Kuomintang members, known as the "Western Hills" group because of the place outside Peking which they chose for their meetings, advocated the expulsion of the communists from the KMT (Kuomintang) and the dismissal of Borodin.

Following the death of Sun, two men, Chiang Kai-shek and Wang Ching-wei, had emerged as possible successors to his leadership. Chiang was soon made commander-in-chief of the army and President of the new Whampoa Military Academy in Canton. Although distrustful of both the CCP and Russia, he realised that Russian assistance was vital if Sun's dream of a military expedition striking north from Canton towards Peking to unify the country was to be realised. Even so, Chiang took advantage of Borodin's temporary absence in Peking during March 1926 to arrest many communists in Canton and to put several Russian advisers under house arrest.

In spite of this action the Comintern insisted that the CCP should maintain its ties with the KMT, and on his return Borodin agreed to restrict the activities of the communists in the KMT and to support Chiang's Northern Expedition. On his side, Chiang promised to restrain the Western Hills group.

With the help of arms supplies and military advisers sent by the Russian government, the Northern Expedition began in July 1926. The troops were aided considerably in their task by the activities of the communists, notably Mao Tse-tung, who agitated among the peasants along the route of the KMT army. Ever since May 1925, from the time of the May Thirtieth Incident (when, following the death of a communist labour organiser, British police fired into a crowd of demonstrators, killing ten) which had kindled a nationalist revolt against the foreigners and the northern warlords for working with them, the peasants, their lives worse under the warlords than under the Manchus, had been in a state of turmoil. The warlord Wu P'ei-fu, entrenched in the Wuhan cities, was hampered by labour discontent, again fomented by the CCP. In the face of the advancing KMT forces, Wu fled north for safety.

Meanwhile Chiang Kai-shek, at the head of a second column, was moving more slowly towards Shanghai. On taking Nanchang, the capital of Kiangsi province, in November, he opted to remain there for the winter.

By the start of 1927, conflict was coming to a head between the left-wing of the KMT headed by Wang Ching-wei and the right-wing under Chiang Kai-shek. The conflict was due to a number of factors: personal rivalry between the two men; differing views on the alliance with the communists; Wang's fear of Chiang's military machine; and the opposition of Borodin, who viewed with disfavour Chiang's advance on Shanghai, which might upset the Western powers. Borodin urged that the KMT should proceed north to Peking.

In January 1927 Wang Ching-wei moved the KMT National Government to Wuhan. Chiang, naturally, would have preferred Nanchang, where his own headquarters were. In March the Wuhan government formally placed restrictions on the military and political authority of Chiang. Undeterred, Chiang moved out of Nanchang, and entered Shanghai the same month, where the workers, organised by the communists under the leadership of the able Chou En-lai, had taken over control of the Chinese section of the city. In the International Concession the foreign business representatives trembled as they saw the revolution reach their doorstep. They

need not have worried, for Chiang Kai-shek, seeing the un-
feasibility of any prolonged unity between the KMT (the party
of the landlords and merchants) and the CCP (the party of
workers and peasants), promptly gained the backing of the
secret societies, and the bankers and other business interests,
and launched a massacre of CCP members and all suspected
communists on 12 April. Chou En-lai himself only escaped by
the skin of his teeth.

At this betrayal by his avowed ally, Stalin, engrossed in his
power conflict with Trotsky (who had been urging the break
of the links between the communists and the Kuomintang),
claimed that the defection of Chiang was a positive step which
had cleansed the KMT of the national bourgeoisie. Stalin now
pinned his hopes for the continuation of the alliance upon the
Left KMT of Wang Ching-wei in Wuhan. The Left KMT re-
affirmed the policy of collaboration. There were now three
governments in China—the recognised government in Peking,
the National Government of the Left KMT in Wuhan, and a
new National Government under Chiang Kai-shek, formed in
Nanking in April.

Friendship between the CCP and the Left KMT did not
continue for long. Wang Ching-wei, suspicious for some time
that the communists planned to capture the KMT, or at least
play a dominant role in it, had his fears confirmed when a
Comintern representative, M. N. Roy, showed him a telegram
from Stalin which urged the CCP to take control of the KMT.
In mid-July the Wuhan government purged the communists
from its midst, and sent the Comintern advisers, including
Borodin, off on the long trek back to Moscow.

Stalin, faced with the abject failure of his policy of working
with the KMT, claimed that the CCP, and especially its leader
Ch'en Tu-hsiu, had deliberately carried out incorrect policies.
In fact the CCP leadership had done the best that it could to
carry out the tasks laid down by the Comintern. Where they
could not completely follow Comintern instructions, for example on the policy of confiscation of the land, it was because they did not have control over the KMT, which was
mainly a party of landlords.

Stalin's policy, which had aimed at a strong, unified China
run by a government friendly to Russia, had failed because

the communists were never able to get organisational control of the KMT—due largely to the success of Borodin in creating a tightly disciplined, Leninist party out of the KMT, run on the same democratic-centralist lines as the Russian Communist Party. Furthermore, Stalin, thousands of miles away in Moscow, was poorly informed about events in China, and underestimated the capacities of Chiang Kai-shek. Lastly, embroiled in his domestic power struggle with Trotsky, Stalin could not give up the policy of the KMT–CCP united front for fear of admitting the validity of Trotsky's arguments.

The communists, their membership decimated, their urban bases of power destroyed, and blamed by Stalin for his own errors, took to the countryside for a refuge, and over the years evolved a strategy independent of the Comintern.

Armed insurrection

Following their decimation in the cities, the CCP Central Committee convened an Emergency Conference in Hankow on 7 August to try to salvage something from the wreckage. The leader of the Party, Ch'en Tu-hsiu, was made the scapegoat for Stalin's errors, and after being condemned for capitulating to the KMT and for his "refusal" to carry out the radical agrarian policies of the Comintern, he was replaced by Ch'ü Ch'iu-pai. The new Party line, based on the principles laid down by the Comintern, laid emphasis on the agrarian revolution, but stressed that it was to be executed under the control of the proletariat. The initial task of the CCP was therefore to organise the working class in the cities. The Comintern also called for armed uprisings in the urban areas to be coordinated with insurrection in the villages.

The first attempt to implement this new line had already taken place a few days earlier, on 1 August, when two communist commanders in the KMT armies, Ho Lung and Yeh T'ing, supported by Chu Teh and others, mutinied at Nanchang, the capital of Kiangsi province, and held the city briefly before being dislodged by KMT troops. Although the communists were soon in full retreat, the anniversary of 1 August is celebrated today as the birth of the Red Army. The creation of this independent communist force had been sanctioned by the Comintern, once it was realised that hope no longer existed for the CCP to capture political control of the KMT and so of the KMT military forces.

At the same time as the urban insurrection at Nanchang, there were attempts to execute the new line in the countryside, of which the most famous were the Autumn Harvest Uprisings in Hunan, which were organised by Mao Tse-tung in September 1927. Mao had been sent to Hunan by the Central Committee to prepare for the Uprisings. The autumn was chosen as the time that the peasants were most likely to support any rebellion, since it was during the autumn harvest that taxes were collected. Mao aimed to confiscate the land of the large and middle landlords, and redistribute it to the poor peasants. He also wanted to organise a revolutionary army, and to organise soviets.

"Soviet" was a term borrowed directly from Russian experience and referred to the representative councils of workers, peasants and soldiers first set up at the time of the 1905 revolution, and later repeated in 1917. In China it later came to refer more generally to any territorial area controlled by the Red Army. Mao prematurely adopted the policy of organising soviets during the Autumn Harvest Uprisings, for although it had been tentatively mooted as a slogan by Stalin in July, it was not actually authorised by the Comintern as a policy until the end of September, by which time the Uprisings had been crushed.

Using four regiments, Mao launched the Uprising on 9 September. The plan was to gain support from the peasants in the rural areas, and then attack the Hunan provincial capital of Changsha. But due to inadequate local support, and military reverses at the hands of KMT troops, the attack on Changsha had to be called off on 15 September, and Mao, with the remnants of his supporters numbering about 1,000, was forced to flee for refuge to the mountain stronghold of Chingkangshan, which he reached in October. Because of the failure of the Uprisings, and for his premature advocacy of organising soviets before they were officially authorised, Mao was removed from his position as a member of the CCP Central Committee in November 1927.

Although they were not successful, the Autumn Harvest Uprisings confirmed Mao's belief in the revolutionary potential of the peasants, which he had first discovered for himself in 1925. This belief of Mao's, one of the basic tenets of "Maoism", is discussed in his well-known Hunan Report, written in early 1927, but based on his findings of the previous year. The Hunan Report articulates his view that it is the peasantry which will eventually defeat imperialism and the Kuomintang. If we are to allot the relative accomplishments in the revolution to date, says Mao, then we must give 70 per cent to the peasants, and only 30 per cent to the urban proletariat and the military.

However true this statement may have been in fact, it was quite contrary to the canons of orthodox Marxism–Leninism, which required that prime reliance be placed on the industrial proletariat. Even though the agrarian revolution might play the major part in the Chinese revolution, it must nevertheless be under the control of the working class, with the peasantry playing a supporting role. The Hunan Report was not therefore a Marxist document, for it entirely ignored the leading role of the proletariat. The Report was not, however, a deliberate deviation from Marxism–Leninism, but rather showed Mao's ignorance of the subject at that time. Nor did it spell out fully the complete principles of the later Maoist revolutionary strategy. There was no mention, for example, of the need for rural base areas. Mao did not yet realise that China was a fragmented nation, which would not be toppled by a revolution in one or two major cities, as had happened in centralised Russia. He only later came to see that in China the revolution required to expand gradually from fixed territorial bases in the countryside.

In the latter half of 1927 Ch'ü Ch'iu-pai, Ch'en Tu-hsiu's replacement as CCP leader, was trying, without much success, to organise the city workers. The campaign of the KMT "white terror", launched against the communists and their sympathisers in the cities, together with the activity of the KMT "yellow" unions, who supported demands by the workers for better pay and conditions instead of outright revolution, had all led to the failure of the proletariat to respond to communist blandishments and the petering out of a number of small strikes.

In spite of this marked apathy, a Central Committee plenum

of November 1927 agreed with the Comintern that the revolution was rising to a new and higher stage. Stalin was pursuing this policy, in the face of all evidence to the contrary, because he needed a victory in China to support him in his struggle against the Trotskyite opposition at home. It was by no accident that the next urban uprising, the ill-fated Canton Commune, was timed to occur in December, while the 15th Congress of the Communist Party of the Soviet Union was under way in Moscow, in spite of the fact that there was clearly little backing for the uprising in Canton.

The Canton Commune, organised by the CCP and Comintern agents, was staged on 11 December with the communists holding the city for only forty-eight hours. The Kuomintang soon retook the city, and quickly and efficiently massacred all those suspected of complicity in the uprising, some 5,000 all told.

This sacrifice by the CCP enabled Stalin to claim the Commune as a victory, but added to the defeats of Nanchang and the Autumn Harvest Uprisings, it was no longer possible to claim that there was a revolutionary rising tide in China. Consequently, a new line was ushered in at the Ninth Plenum of the Executive Committee of the Comintern (ECCI) convened in February 1928. The Plenum, as was now customary, denounced the Chinese leadership for Stalin's responsibilities. Ch'ü Ch'iu-pai was condemned for putschism and for "playing with insurrection". The new line spoke of China as being in a trough between two revolutionary waves. A new revolutionary wave was imminent, and would arrive at some unspecified time in the future. Meanwhile, the CCP was urged to build soviets.

Building soviets was just what Mao was doing at that time on Chingkangshan, although in retreating there for safety at the end of 1927, he had acted independently of instructions from either Moscow or Shanghai. Moreover, it was on Chingkangshan that the strategy began to be developed that was to lead the communists to ultimate victory.

Chingkangshan was an inaccessible mountain range on the borders of Hunan and Kiangsi. Being on the borders of two provinces, both sets of authorities tended to leave the settlement of any disturbance to the other. It was in consequence a well-known hideout for brigands, and indeed Mao, on his arrival, united with two bandit chiefs and incorporated their men into his army. In April 1928 Mao was joined by Chu Teh, bringing with him the remnants of some of the forces that had mutinied at Nanchang. The Red Army now comprised a force of about 10,000 men, of whom 4,000 had rifles. Together they set up local soviets, and executed a radical land policy of liquidating the landlords and redistributing the land of the whole area.

That summer of 1928 both the Sixth Congress of the CCP and the Sixth Congress of the Comintern were held in Moscow. Ch'ü Ch'iu-pai, already in disgrace, was formally replaced by Hsiang Chung-fa, a former boatman, and one of the few genuine proletarians in the Chinese communist leadership. Lacking in ability and intelligence, power in fact devolved on to the shoulders of Li Li-san, an experienced labour organiser. The line laid down for the CCP at the Sixth Congress confirmed that the agrarian revolution was the main content of the Chinese revolution, but that the recapturing of the Party's proletarian bases in the cities had first priority. It was deemed essential to link the rural soviets to the struggles of the urban workers, and to establish Party control over the peasants.

The Sixth Congress also sanctioned the guerrilla warfare being carried on by Mao and Chu in the mountains, as indeed it was virtually forced to, bearing in mind that the activities of Mao and Chu were the only successful operations in progress. The Congress nevertheless laid down a line which was contrary to Mao's thinking on a number of issues. The Congress stressed the need for proletarian hegemony over the revolution, while Mao emphasised the peasants. The Congress also spoke of preparations for armed uprisings in the future, while Mao urged gradual expansion and consolidation of the rural base areas.

In November 1928 the Mao-Chu army on Chingkangshan was reinforced by the troops of P'eng Teh-huai, a communist and former regimental commander during the Northern Expedition, who had rebelled against the KMT. In spite of these additional forces, Mao and Chu were obliged to leave Chingkangshan in January 1929, because they were suffering militarily from KMT attacks, and economically from the KMT blockade. After a fierce battle, they set up a new base in south Kiangsi which was to become the future Chinese Soviet Republic.

In spite of his inability to establish himself on Chingkang-shan, Mao's experience there confirmed his belief in the necessity of rural base areas, which he said were to an army as buttocks were to a person—both essential for rest and re-cuperation.[1] All the elements of the Maoist strategy were now apparent—the use of rural base areas (soviets) from which to conduct land reform and guerrilla warfare by means of a Red Army led by a disciplined communist party.

From early 1929, in south Kiangsi, Mao began having more success than hitherto, largely because his more moder-ate agrarian policies were beginning to pay dividends in terms of peasant support. But at the same time, the Central Com-mittee in Shanghai under Li Li-san was trying to carry out the line of the Sixth Congress, and was deciding policies concerning the role of the soviet areas which were in con-flict with the views of Mao.

During the latter half of 1928, and early 1929, Li Li-san had failed, in the face of general apathy, to successfully organ-ise the workers of the cities. But in the summer of 1929, because the Comintern announced that a new revolutionary high tide in China was imminent, Li was also forced to declare that he "saw" a new high tide, where in fact none existed. In October, Moscow, partially because it viewed the economic depression in the United States as symptomatic of a global phenomenon, confirmed the existence of a rising tide of revolution in China. Li, desperately anxious not to miss this tide, faced the situation of communist weakness in the cities, balanced by considerable successes of the rural Red Armies at the end of 1929 and the start of 1930.

For Li, always an urban worker, the cities were the brains and heart of the ruling class, whereas the villages were but appendages. The way to victory was therefore to be had by seizing the cities. In January 1930 he confirmed the existence of a rising tide in China, and decided to harness the soviet

[1] Stuart R. Schram, *Mao Tse-tung* (Harmondsworth, Middx.: Pelican Books Ltd, 1966), p. 136.

areas to help him strike at the cities. This would be accomplished, reasoned Li, by starting urban uprisings which would expand into the countryside, where they would be supported by the Red Army, operating from its guerrilla bases. Li correctly saw that China had no one single political or administrative centre, and so he advocated initial victories in one or more provinces.

In June 1930 this line subtly but significantly changed. Li now reasoned that if the Red Army was going to be used in conjunction with urban uprisings there would be no harm in ordering the Red Army to attack the cities, and thus spark off the revolutionary situation which was supposed to exist there. This policy, the kernel of the so-called "Li Li-san line", was sanctioned by the Comintern, and Li ordered the Red Armies (now made up of some 65,000 men) to attack Changsha, Wuhan and Nanchang. Changsha was captured at the end of July and held for ten days. The other attacks failed, and a second attempt to take Changsha in September was unsuccessful after Mao, who had never favoured wasting his troops on premature attacks on the cities, commanded his forces to withdraw back to the south Kiangsi base area.

There had, of course, to be an inquest to settle the responsibility for the failures of the Li Li-san line. The former CCP leader Ch'ü Ch'iu-pai was sent from Moscow to condemn Li at the Third Plenum of the Central Committee, convened at the end of September. Ch'ü found it extremely difficult to make any deep criticisms of Li, partly because there was in fact little difference between the Comintern line and the policies that Li had carried out thus making it very awkward to attack Li and avoid criticising the Comintern at the same time, and partly because Li had the backing of a strong party machine behind him, and included Chou En-lai among his supporters. The Third Plenum therefore confirmed Li Li-san in power, while finding him guilty of only tactical rather than major strategic errors.

This situation did not continue for long. The Comintern agent in China, Pavel Mif, at that time Stalin's leading "China expert", was infuriated that the Third Plenum had not unseated Li. Mif was accompanied by a group of young students recently returned to China from several years in the

Soviet Union. The Returned Student Group, or the "Twenty-eight Bolsheviks" as they were ironically called, were able theorists, but quite lacking in practical revolutionary experience. Nevertheless, Mif intended to hand over the leadership of the CCP to them.

In November 1930 the CCP received a letter from the Comintern, which, drawing on the ambiguities of its own previous directives, condemned Li Li-san for major errors of line. Li was unable to withstand this assault, resigned, and went to Moscow "to study". He remained there until 1946, when he returned to China in the wake of the brief Soviet occupation of Manchuria. At the Fourth Plenum of the Central Committee held in January 1931, the Returned Student Group was confirmed in power, with their members occupying the leading positions. The three chief members of the group were Ch'en Shao-yü (alias Wang Ming), Ch'in Pang-hsien (Po Ku), and Chang Wen-t'ien (Lo Fu).

While the battle for the leadership of the Central Committee was being fought out in Shanghai, Mao had been consolidating his own position in the soviet areas by arresting and possibly shooting some 3,000 supporters of Li Li-san in the Fut'ien Incident of December 1930. The Returned Student Group, however, like Li Li-san, were seeking to bring the soviet areas under their own control. They were also, during 1931, occupied with drawing up policies for the soviet areas with which Mao disagreed, particularly with their policies on military and agrarian affairs.

In addition to this intra-Party conflict, Mao was also faced with a wave of Kuomintang "Bandit Encirclement Campaigns" initiated at the end of 1930. Chiang Kai-shek, alarmed by the Red Army strikes against the cities in the summer of 1930, determined to wipe them out once and for all. However, the first two of his Encirclement Campaigns had been defeated by the Red Armies, using guerrilla warfare. The third campaign, headed by Chiang himself, was faring better, and in the summer of 1931 it looked as though Juichin, the soviet headquarters in Kiangsi, was in danger of being overrun. But the Japanese, by creating the Mukden Incident of 18 September 1931 and occupying Manchuria, fortuitously distracted Chiang's attention. Chiang was forced to call off the campaigns, and did not resume them for two years,[2] during which time the soviet areas reached the peak of their development.

While Mao was consolidating his position in the Central Soviet Area of south Kiangsi during the spring and summer of 1931, both the Returned Student Group and the Comintern were devising policies for the rural bases which were contrary to those advocated by him. This conflict, which was carried on by means of several directives sent from Shanghai, calling on Mao to change his military and agrarian tactics, was exacerbated when the Central Committee, its activities hindered by KMT police activity, began to transfer to the soviet areas as from the summer of 1931. Chou En-lai went to Juichin, and arrived there by the end of the year. Other Central Committee-men, such as Chang Kuo-t'ao and Shen Tse-min, moved to the second largest soviet of Oyüwan, on the borders of Hupeh, Honan and Anhwei, during 1931, while Wang Ming went to Moscow at about the same time. Po Ku and Lo Fu both arrived in Juichin in 1932.

The First Party Conference of the Soviet Areas was convened in November 1931, and denounced Mao's moderate land policies as a "rich peasant line", under which the benefits of land reform had accrued, not to the poor and middle peasants, but to the rich peasants, who had also succeeded in worming their way into the organs of soviet administration. On military policies, Mao's guerrilla tactics were condemned as being unsuitable for large-scale warfare and the need to secure initial victories in one or more provinces.

Surprisingly, the laws and policies adopted by the First National Soviet Congress, which was convened in Juichin on 7 November 1931 (the anniversary of the Russian Revolution), and which followed immediately on the heels of the Party Conference, were by no means hostile to Mao. Furthermore, the leading organs of the government elected at the Congress were all controlled by Mao and his supporters, with members of the Returned Student Group in a subordinate role. The explanation is probably that Mao's machine was

[2] The Fourth Campaign began in June 1932 but did not reach the Central Soviet Area until February 1933.

entrenched in the soviet areas, and in command of the electoral procedure for selecting delegates to the Congress. Mao could well have manipulated the elections so as to produce a gathering of delegates responsive to his wishes.

In addition to passing a Land Law, Labour Law and other resolutions concerning the Red Army and economic development, it can be said that the First National Soviet Congress, which formally created the Chinese Soviet Republic and elected Mao as its Chairman, institutionalised the shift of the CCP from the city to the countryside, where it was to remain for over fifteen years.

It was on the basis of the institutions set up at this Congress, and the methods with which they were operated during the 1931–4 period, that the CCP gained much of its experience that was utilised in later years in the "liberated areas" and in post-1949 Communist China.

In the late spring of 1932 Chiang Kai-shek, pursuing his policy of deferring the fight against Japan until he had defeated his enemies at home, launched the Fourth "Bandit Encirclement Campaign". By the summer of 1932, the 100,000 troops deployed by the KMT had liquidated the Hunan–Hupeh soviet area under the command of Ho Lung, and Oyüwan was hard-pressed. In October Chang Kuo-t'ao and his forces were forced to flee from Oyüwan and seek refuge in Szechuan.

In the face of these reverses the CCP convened a meeting at Ningtu, Kiangsi, in August 1932 to discuss military strategy. According to Mao, who attended the Conference, it continued the erroneous policies decided at the Fourth Plenum of the Central Committee in January 1931. Mao favoured a policy of mobile guerrilla warfare, and the luring of the enemy deep into soviet territory before launching a surprise counter-attack. This was clearly not conducive to the maintenance of a high morale among the population of the Chinese Soviet Republic, who had to endure their territory being overrun, apparently without any hindrance from the Red Army. Mao's views were attacked as being obsolescent, and Mao himself clashed with Chou En-lai who, backed by the Central Committee and encouraged by the growth of the Red Army, advocated positional warfare, capturing the cities, and taking the war into enemy territory. The views of Chou En-lai prevailed, and Mao, according to his own testimony, devoted himself almost entirely to governmental work from October 1932 onwards, while Chou became political commissar over the Red Army in May 1933.

The fact that the new strategy proved successful against Chiang's Fourth Campaign reinforced the belief of the Party leaders that Mao's guerrilla tactics were obsolete. Mao was later (1945) to claim that the Fourth Campaign was only defeated because his influence in the Red Army had not been completely eradicated at that time, and that the defeat inflicted on the Red Army by the Fifth and final Campaign, and the consequent loss of the Kiangsi base, were due in large part to the use of the incorrect strategy. This chronology allows Mao to reap the credit for the successes against the first four campaigns, while absolving him from blame for the loss of the soviet areas. It is doubtful however, whether the adoption of Mao's guerrilla methods would have made any difference to the final result.

In August 1933, rested and equipped with German military advisers, Chiang Kai-shek's force of one million men began the Fifth Campaign against the communists, using a system of slow strangulation by economic blockade, while drawing tighter the noose of concrete blockhouses, constructed as they advanced. In the middle of this campaign there was convened the Second National Soviet Congress, which met in January 1934 and re-elected the personnel of the soviet government. This Congress formalised the control of the Returned Student leadership over the government, so that they now controlled all three power bases—Party, army and government—in the soviet areas. Their supporters were dominant in the key organs of the government, with many of Mao's henchmen dismissed or demoted. Mao himself remained as Chairman of the Soviet Republic in return for his public acquiescence in the policies of the Party leadership.

The Second Congress closed prematurely after only a few days because of news of a worsening situation on the military front. As the year wore on, the hardship in the soviet areas increased as the blockade tightened, and the Red Army suffered defeats. By September, less than 10 per cent of the original counties forming the Central Soviet Area were still in soviet hands. The decision to leave Kiangsi and seek safety elsewhere had been taken early that summer, and in mid-October 1934 the body of the Red Army, numbering some 100,000 men, broke out of the KMT blockade, and headed westwards on the first stage of the epic Long March.

The Long March, an historic epic of endurance, lasted just over one year, during which time the Red Army travelled 6,000 miles crossing 12 provinces, 24 rivers, and 18 mountain ranges (five of them permanently snow-capped). With few halts for rest, they maintained an average of 24 miles per day, on foot. In the initial stages of the march, as they passed through Kwangtung and Kwangsi, they suffered considerable losses at the hands of hostile troops. When they reached Tsunyi, in Kweichow province, during January 1935, an expanded meeting of the CCP Political Bureau (Politburo) was called, at which Mao castigated the Returned Student leaders, blaming them for the loss of the Kiangsi base and the reverses sustained on the retreat. He apparently obtained wide support (including the backing of the mercurial Chou En-lai), and while Po Ku stepped down from the post of Secretary General in favour of Lo Fu, Mao moved up to the new position of Chairman of the Politburo. Mao was now the leader of the CCP.

However, he was not without opposition. Moving west and then north from Tsunyi, in September the Red Army met up with the forces of Chang Kuo-t'ao at Maoerhkai in Szechuan. Chang was a member of the Politburo, and commanded a much larger force than Mao's remnants from the Kiangsi base. Differences of opinion existed between the two, with Chang claiming that soviets were inappropriate for China, and proposing to head for Sikang province, so as to be closer to Russian influence. Mao favoured continuing north to the remaining soviet base in north Shensi, there to establish an anti-Japanese presence.

The two men were unable to reconcile their differences, and so they split up in August 1935, with Chang Kuo-t'ao heading west, and Mao crossing the Grasslands—a cold, treacherous and muddy swamp—to reach north Shensi in

October 1935. There the communists made their capital at Pao-an, until it transferred to Yenan in December 1936.

Chang Kuo-t'ao, his westward march eventually abandoned, rejoined Mao in October 1936. He was subsequently expelled from the CCP in 1938 and went over to the Kuomintang. He now lives in Hong Kong. The total troops available to the communists at the end of 1936 numbered only 30,000 from the 300,000 they had had in the summer of 1934. It seemed that one last push from Chiang Kai-shek would force them to seek refuge in the north, crossing the border to exile in the Soviet Union.

Proposals for a Second United Front with the Kuomintang
In August 1935 Mao Tse-tung initiated new proposals for a united front with the KMT against Japanese aggression. In addition to being a tactical move designed to give the CCP a respite from further military campaigns directed against them by KMT forces, the CCP also genuinely wished to drive the Japanese out of China. These proposals were backed by the Comintern, which wished to use the KMT armies to act as a bulwark in the event of a Japanese attack on the Soviet Union. The CCP initiative for a united front therefore was in harmony with the general line of the international communist movement at that time, which was for a world-wide united front to defend Russia against fascism.

These proposals, although they were welcomed by many among the Chinese intellectual community, were rejected by Chiang Kai-shek during 1935 and 1936. The situation only changed following the Sian Incident of December 1936.

Sian was the capital of Shensi province, and the base from which KMT troops were to launch their attack on the CCP. The KMT troops were primarily from Manchuria and under the command of Chang Hsüeh-liang, the son of the former warlord of Manchuria, Chang Tso-lin. Among these forces, feeling ran high that it was better that they should return to drive the Japanese enemy out of Manchuria, than fight against their brother Chinese, and a virtual cease fire had been agreed between them and the communists. Chiang Kai-shek, who flew up to Sian to investigate the situation, was kidnapped by his own troops, and only released, following the intervention of Chou En-lai as a mediator, when he agreed to stop his attacks on the communists, and to put into operation a united front against Japan. For this, his life was spared, and the CCP in turn agreed to recognise him as head of state, to rename their soviet the Shensi—Kansu—Ninghsia Border Area, to suspend the confiscation of the landlords' land, and to call the Red Army the Eighth Route Army, under the command of Chiang Kai-shek. Because of these concessions by the CCP, Chiang Kai-shek saved face, but in fact he had agreed to all the major demands of the CCP.

Following the united front agreement, the Eighth Route Army was organised under Chu Teh with 30,000 men, and another force, the new Fourth Army, was formed in east China with 10,000 men under Yeh T'ing. The CCP muted its criticism of the KMT and Chiang Kai-shek, at least during the initial stages of the alliance, and the Soviet Union sent considerable military supplies to the KMT.

On 7 July 1937 the Japanese, using an incident at the Marco Polo Bridge near Peking as an excuse, started a widespread assault on China. With big superiority in equipment and training, they quickly took Peking that same month. Shanghai fell in November, and the Wuhan cities and Canton were occupied by October 1938. The KMT refused to surrender, and moved their capital to Chungking, Szechuan province, in the west of China. The Japanese therefore held all the coastline, the north China plain and the Yangtze valley, but because of their rapid advance, and shortage of men, were only able to hold the major cities and lines of communication, and were unable to secure vast areas of the countryside, which were left open to communist guerrilla activity.

The CCP, expanding into the vacuum left in the rural areas by the Japanese, set up a number of border region governments in the areas which they controlled during the late thirties and early forties—bases which flourished due to both brutal Japanese repression and CCP organisation. As in Kiangsi, the administration was in the form of a pyramidal structure of people's councils, although from March 1940, a modification was introduced with the implementation of the "three-thirds" rule, which stipulated that on the people's councils, only one-third of the members were to be CCP members, with one-third non-party "progressives" and one-third "middle-of-the-roaders" such as enlightened gentry. Since the progressives could always be relied upon to vote with the communists, effective power always remained with the CCP. Nevertheless, the system encouraged rudimentary political participation by the peasants, and helped to win their support. The population also warmed to the communists because of their very moderate land policies, under which only the land of landlords who collaborated with the Japanese was confiscated, with the remainder receiving both rent and interest. The peasants gained by rent reductions and fixed taxes.

The land programme of the CCP was so moderate that the Party was often thought of as a collection of agrarian reformers, although in fact its aim of a communist China was never abandoned, but only put on one side temporarily as a tactical measure. The theoretical formulation for these moderate policies and the alliance with the KMT was put forward by Mao in his *On New Democracy,* published in 1940, which made China a part of the new democratic revolution, which was not the same as the old bourgeois-democratic revolution, since it was led by a joint "revolutionary-democratic dictatorship" of several classes, which included other political parties, and the intellectuals.

In addition to the problems posed by the Japanese, the communists were facing serious internal problems. There was great difficulty in coordinating the activities of the scattered border region governments, and communication was hampered by bad geographical conditions. Secondly, the CCP was in danger of being diluted because of a tremendous influx of new members—membership rose from 40,000 in 1937 to 1,200,000 in 1945. This resulted in a lowering of standards, a shortage of members with a thorough ideological background, and the inclusion in the Party of many intellectuals who had been attracted to Yenan from elsewhere in China, and who brought with them either ideals of Western liberalism or who were aware of the contradiction between the Marxist model of an urban proletarian communist party and the peasant organisation they found in the hills of Shensi.

To stiffen Party discipline and restore ideological orthodoxy, and to create uniformity of action in the scattered border governments by having decisions made by Party members acting alike because they drew their conclusions from identical theoretical assumptions, the CCP inaugurated the *cheng-feng* or rectification movement in early 1942. This movement consisted primarily of using small groups to study the works of Mao Tse-tung, Marx, Engels, Lenin and Stalin. Party branches made an investigation of their work, and Party members criticised each other and indulged in self-criticism. Some were dismissed and others made to reform.

The *cheng-feng* movement also represented Mao's final consolidation of power within the CCP, for it was directed against dogmatism within the Party, in particular the slavish imitation of Russian methods. The main target was Wang Ming (Ch'en Shao-yü), the former Returned Student Group leader, who had gone back to the Soviet Union in 1931, and had returned to China in 1937. Marxism became sinified, or placed in a Chinese context. It was no longer the case that a communist had to be from a proletarian background—providing that he was imbued with the correct proletarian *ideology*, then he was a true communist, representing the interests of the proletariat, even though he himself was originally a peasant. The *cheng-feng* movement restored ideological orthodoxy and discipline to the Party, and at the Seventh Party Congress in 1945, Mao emerged as undisputed leader.

The Japanese and the Kuomintang

From 1938 onwards, a virtual stalemate existed in the conflict between the Japanese, and the KMT now based in Chungking, with only scattered action over a wide front. During the remainder of the war, until 1945, the KMT did not launch a single major offensive. Cut off from the richer and more industrialised areas of the country, the KMT became more reactionary and corrupt, and morale gradually declined.

However, capitalising on the hatred of the Japanese aroused by the rough treatment of the civilian population, the communists mobilised the peasants and set up their guerrilla bases behind the Japanese lines, where their armies and influence grew while the KMT stagnated in the cities. Breakdowns in the united front appeared with armed clashes between the KMT and CCP, as the KMT saw the communists, harness-

ing Chinese nationalism to their cause, becoming identified
with and leading the resistance to the Japanese invader.

With the KMT attack on the Shensi–Kansu–Ninghsia
border area in 1939–40, the united front existed only in
name. The situation further deteriorated after the New Fourth
Army Incident of January 1941, when it was attacked by
the KMT, suffering heavy losses, after the KMT accused the
communists of trying to organise guerrilla bases in "their"
area of south-east China.

From this time on, both sides began making preparations
to liquidate the other, once the Japanese were disposed of.
The KMT sat in Chungking, and waited for the USA (which
was now an active participant in the war following the Japanese attack on Pearl Harbour in December 1941) to drive the
enemy out of China. Much US aid to the KMT was never
used against the Japanese, but hoarded to fight the communists once the war was over. Furthermore, for fear of arming
the peasants, the KMT never undertook any guerrilla operations against the enemy. However, by their refusal to surrender, the KMT did keep a large number of Japanese troops
stationed in China, who would otherwise have been liberated
to play a more active role elsewhere.

On their side the communists also gave a major part of
their activities to expanding the area of the territory they
controlled, and the size of the army. By 1945, they controlled
an area of a quarter of a million square miles, with an army
at least half a million strong. Their territory comprised fifteen
"liberated areas" throughout nineteen provinces, with a population of 100 million, or 25 per cent of China's total population.

The war had sapped the vitality of the KMT. Military in-
activity, and a corrupt administration, coupled with inflation
and general wartime scarcities, had led to a serious decline
in morale. Nevertheless, their army of almost four million
men was both larger and better equipped than that of the
communists.

The dropping of atom-bombs on Hiroshima and Nagasaki,
and the resulting surrender of Japan in August 1945, caught
both sides in China by surprise—particularly the KMT, who
had always awaited a US landing on the coast of China

against the occupying Japanese. The result was a rush by the CCP and the KMT to obtain the arms and territory surrendered by the enemy.

Chiang Kai-shek, as commander of all Allied forces in the China area, requested the US Air Force to fly his troops to the northern cities, so that they, and not the CCP, would receive the surrender of the Japanese. Half a million KMT troops were air-lifted to Wuhan, Peking and Tientsin, so that the KMT occupied the major cities of North China, with the CCP in command of the countryside, and advancing into Inner Mongolia, Shansi and Manchuria. The Russians had occupied Manchuria in August after declaring war on Japan that same month. By doing so, they recouped the privileges there that they had lost in the Russo-Japanese War of 1905, a provision which had been agreed to by the "Big Three" meeting of Churchill, Roosevelt and Stalin at Yalta in February 1945, but kept secret from China.

Russia was now in a position to give control over Manchuria, and its industrial resources, to the CCP, had it so desired. However, not only did this not take place, but the Russians remained in occupation in Manchuria longer than they had anticipated, at the request of Chiang Kai-shek, so that he could have time to get his troops there. When the Russians did withdraw, a large part of the arms captured from the Japanese did find their way into the hands of the communist armies, but most of Manchuria's industry was dismantled and shipped back to the Soviet Union. The situation after the Soviet withdrawal was similar to that in North China, with the KMT occupying the major cities and lines of communication, and the communists dominant in the countryside, where they succeeded in cutting the north–south rail links, so that the KMT garrisons had to be supplied by air. In Central and East China, a reverse situation existed, with the CCP only occupying a few isolated enclaves, surrounded by the KMT.

Civil war

Negotiations had started as early as 1943, and US Ambassador Hurley had talked to Mao at Yenan in 1944. In August Mao went with Hurley to Chungking, and conferred with Chiang Kai-shek, which produced an agreement of little real value, since no agreement could be reached on key issues concerning a possible coalition government, the communist base areas, and command of the armed forces.

A further effort was made in December 1945 when President Truman sent General George C. Marshall to negotiate a reconciliation between the two sides. A cease-fire agreement was reached in January 1946, but was short-lived, as both sides were pursuing mutually incompatible aims immersed in the bitterness of two decades of civil war, and each thought they had the ability to defeat the other. The civil war restarted with large-scale battles in Central China in mid-1946, and Marshall, unable to make further progress, left the country in early 1947.

A final US initiative was made in July 1947, when President Truman sent Lieutenant-General Albert C. Wedemeyer to review the state of affairs. Wedemeyer reported that the situation of the KMT could only be improved if they implemented urgent reforms. Inflation was reaching astronomical proportions, alienating those living on fixed incomes, and further corrupting the civil service with graft. The reactionary leadership of the KMT was rapidly losing them much popular support. Up until mid-1947, however, the KMT appeared to be doing well in the military sphere, with a much larger army than the CCP, and, thanks to US aid, one that was superior in arms and equipment. Many CCP dominated areas were recaptured by the KMT forces and their capital of Yenan was overrun in March 1947.

Chiang Kai-shek then over-extended himself (against US advice) by trying simultaneously to reconquer Shantung (so as to reopen the Peking–Tientsin–Nanking railway) and drive the communists out of Manchuria. His campaign in Shantung failed, and he found himself isolated in the cities of Manchuria, while his forces were nibbled away by surprise attacks conducted by the communist forces, who had been consolidated by Lin Piao during the winter of 1946–7.

The year 1947 was the beginning of the end for the Kuomintang. In Manchuria their garrisons were besieged in Mukden and Changchun, short of food and supplies. South of the Yangtze the economic situation continued to deteriorate

and with the general decline in morale the KMT armies lost
the will to fight. In the autumn of 1948 Chiang landed an
armoured division on the Manchurian coast in an attempt
to relieve the beleaguered garrison of Mukden. The relieving
forces were quickly surrounded by the People's Liberation
Army (as the Red Army was now renamed) and surrendered. The Mukden garrison, setting out to relieve it, was
also surrounded and surrendered, giving half a million men,
and their equipment, to the PLA.

Sweeping south, the PLA obtained the surrender of Peking
in January 1949. There was a brief hiatus while Chiang Kai-
shek stepped down from the presidency in order to allow Li
Tsung-jen as acting president to negotiate with the communists on a proposed division of China at the Yangtze, the
lines of the former Sung dynasty. This proposal was quickly
rejected and the communists crossed the Yangtze in April,
capturing Nanking that month, with Shanghai falling in May.
The KMT retreated first to Canton, and then sought final
refuge on Taiwan in December 1949.

The PLA completed "mopping-up" operations by taking
over Hainan Island in early 1950 and destroying a number
of KMT remnants in the south and south-west during the
year, finally overrunning Tibet during 1950–1. Meanwhile,
Mao Tse-tung proclaimed the establishment of the People's
Republic of China in Peking on 1 October 1949.

Great changes were to take place in China after 1949, but
in some respects the triumph of the Communist Party can
be seen as a return to the pre-capitalist period before the
involvement with the Western powers, back to the tradition
of public rather than private enterprise, and rule by a non-
hereditary bureaucratic élite.

2

THE CHINESE COMMUNIST PARTY

Introduction

Communist ideology justifies and legitimates the right of a communist party to a monopoly of political power. For Marx, the dictatorship of the proletariat represented an intermediate stage between capitalism and communism, to which Lenin added the concept of an intellectual élite (the party) needed to give leadership to the working class. The dictatorship of the proletariat in communist China, called the "people's democratic dictatorship", is considered by the Chinese Communist Party to be truly democratic, since it is the dictatorship of the vast majority, the "people", over a tiny minority of reactionaries.

The CCP has as its mission the creation of a stateless, classless society. Because the dictatorship of the proletariat must be led by the party of the proletariat, the CCP by virtue of being the vanguard of the working class, and because of its knowledge of Marxism–Leninism and its organisational capacities, is best able to understand and realise the interests of all the people. By definition, therefore, the interests of the Party are the interests of the people.

The Party, however, conceives of itself not as an administrative body, but as a leadership organ, deciding policies to be implemented by the state structure, and supervising the execution of these policies.

The CCP is the guiding force behind all major policies to be adopted by state and society in China. At the highest levels of the country's major institutions, the Party, government and military, the leaders of these organisations form a series of interlocking directorates to ensure that Party policies will be carried out. Therefore, parallel to the various departments of the CCP Central Committee correspond the staff offices of the State Council (or Cabinet), each supervising a "system" or broad functional area of policy (such as Culture and Education, or Finance and Trade), and each headed by a member of the Central Committee. All members of the "inner cabinet" of the State Council, the most important government organ, will themselves be members of the Party's Central Committee. Similarly, at all levels, the Party apparatus parallels the governmental bureaucracy (as well as every other organisation in society), and exercises leadership over it by means of a Party fraction. The Party fraction in a government organ will be made up of the leading Party members in that organ, who are subject to Party discipline, and make the government responsive to Party commands.

The Thought of Mao Tse-tung

According to Peking, Mao Tse-tung[1] has taken his place with Lenin and Marx in the pantheon of communist heroes. Mao is held to have concretely synthesised Marxism–Leninism with the experience of the Chinese revolution, so that "the epoch of Marx and Engels was one for making preparations for the proletarian revolution, the epoch of Lenin and Stalin was one in which socialist revolution gained victory in one country and a breach was opened on the battlefront of imperialism, and the epoch today is an epoch of Mao Tse-tung in which the world revolutionary victory is to be attained and capitalism and imperialism are to be sent to their tombs".[2]

The Thought of Mao Tse-tung was explicitly enshrined in the 1945 Constitution of the CCP. Omitted from the 1956 Constitution, it has been replaced, and re-emphasised in the new Party constitution ratified at the Ninth Party Congress of April 1969. Mao is therefore held to be a philosopher of great originality, and to be the only living successor to the great communist theoreticians of the past. With the advent of the Cultural Revolution, to the veneration of the Thought of Mao Tse-tung must be added veneration of the man himself with Mao being transmogrified into a God-like figure standing above both people and Party.

[1] Mao's name is now spelled in English by Peking without the hyphen, so as to raise him to grammatical equality with Marx and Lenin, in the phrase Marxism–Leninism–Mao Tsetung Thought.

[2] *Hunan Daily*, 4 February 1966.

Most of Peking's claims are grossly over-exaggerated. Virtually all Mao's philosophical tenets have been put forward at some previous time by Lenin, Stalin or later Soviet writers although Mao has revised certain parts and stressed others. Most of the claims for Mao's originality, therefore, must rest on his practical leadership of a guerrilla war waged from rural base areas, a technique which the Chinese view as being applicable to most underdeveloped countries of the world. For Mao, theory has always been primarily instrumental.

In essence, Maoism is a combination of factors stemming from Mao's life experiences—his chauvinism being based on an early commitment to Chinese nationalism following his awareness of the humiliation and subjugation of China by the West, and his belief in the ability of human will and human action (rather than numbers of men or machines) to be victorious against all odds, together with the trait of "military romanticism", stemming from his almost quarter of a century of armed struggle against the Nationalists and the Japanese. But with the experiences of the Great Leap Forward and the Cultural Revolution, it is becoming increasingly clear that these characteristics run counter to the demands of economic development. Just as China found in the nineteenth century that she could not adopt the machines of the barbarians without modifying her political and social structure, so today industrialisation and economic power bring with them their own logic, which is not congruent with the simple and uncomplicated guerrilla days of old.

Party membership

From the small band of fifty discontented intellectuals who made up the total membership of the CCP at the time of its founding in 1921, the Party grew to some seventeen million by 1961. The initial growth of the Party was slow, and by 1925 its adherents still numbered less than 1,000. Better times were on hand, however, with the advent of the first United Front with the KMT, and by the spring of 1927 membership had leapt to 58,000—only to be drastically and violently reduced to less than a fifth of that figure by the ruthless purging of the CCP from the ranks of the Kuomintang in the summer of that year. Fleeing for refuge into the country-side, the communists recuperated and recruited among the peasants of the Chinese Soviet Republic, so that membership stood at 300,000 by the summer of 1934, although this fig-ure was not to be maintained for long, as the flight of the CCP on the Long March left only a tenth of that number as exhausted remnants in the hills of Shensi a year later. Nevertheless, from that time on the CCP went from strength to strength. Capitalising on the hatred felt by the Chinese for the Japanese occupation troops after 1937, and the desire of the peasants for land ownership, the communists were able, by their resistance to the Japanese and by a programme of agrarian reform, to increase Party membership to 1.2 million by 1945. This figure grew steadily during the ensuing civil war against the forces of Chiang Kai-shek, and in 1949, with victory accomplished, the communists were 4½ million strong.

The initial period of communist consolidation of their rule on the mainland was one of slow growth in party member-ship, for the emphasis was now on quality not quantity, and recruiting standards were altered to favour the working class, rather than the peasantry, so as to create an urban proletarian base. The CCP, for almost a quarter of a century a rural party, had now encircled and occupied the cities. In general, peasant recruitment was only encouraged in the newly lib-erated rural areas where the CCP was weak.

By 1954, there were 6½ million CCP members. In 1955 recruitment policy underwent another change, this time in response to the decision to collectivise agriculture. Clearly, the establishment of agricultural cooperatives required that the Party have a strong rural organisation, and the Party once again opened its doors to the peasants, with member-ship totalling 10.7 million by 1956. Recruitment slowed a little for the 1956–7 period, but soon rose again with the in-auguration of the Great Leap Forward and the establish-ment of rural communes.

There were seventeen million Party members in 1961, the last year for which membership statistics were issued. In all probability, recruiting slowed after the failures of the Great

Leap, and the CCP may well have begun to shrink in size, with the period of the Cultural Revolution hastening the decline.

Membership characteristics

The CCP is overwhelmingly composed of members who joined the Party after 1949. Even in 1961, it was estimated that 80 per cent of its membership joined after "liberation", a figure which will have increased substantially by this time. By contrast, the ruling circles of the Party are still dominated by men who have been in the Party at least since the early 1930s, and who continue to monopolise the ruling positions. This enforced lack of mobility for younger Party members has given rise to the concept of the "generation gap" between the leadership and the rank-and-file, which remains a continuing problem. Even as long ago as 1956 it was estimated that 25 per cent of the CCP was under age twenty-five, and 92 per cent was forty-five or younger, leaving only 8 per cent of the total membership aged forty-six and above.

In 1956 the CCP comprised 1.74 per cent of the total population of the country, with Party members being distributed unevenly—the percentage being rather higher than this in the cities and lower in the countryside. Even assuming that the 1961 figure of seventeen million members has remained stationary (which is unlikely), then given a current population of 700 million, the figure is only 2.43 per cent of Party to population. This would be the lowest of all communist countries, where Party membership tends to increase as the level of industrialisation rises.

According to the new Party constitution adopted in 1969, the CCP is open to "any Chinese worker, poor peasant, lower-middle peasant, revolutionary armyman or any other revolutionary element who has reached the age of eighteen". Any intending applicant must be recommended by two Party members and have his application considered by the local Party branch, who will "seek the opinions of the broad masses inside and outside the Party". Although the route to full membership is not spelt out in any detail in the 1969 Constitution, the normal situation would be for the individual to be placed on probation if his application was accepted by the Party branch and approved by the Party committee on the next higher level. During the probationary period of up to two years, assigned Party members would cultivate him so as to learn his history and attitudes, following which his application would again be brought up in the branch meeting.

The Party's major source for new members is the Young Communist League. In addition, the Party draws heavily on those who distinguish themselves as "activists" in one of the mass campaigns launched periodically throughout the country.

Once in the Party, members are expected to "study and apply Marxism–Leninism–Mao Tsetung Thought in a living way; work for the interests of the vast majority of the people of China and the world; and be able at uniting with the great majority, including those who have wrongly opposed them but are sincerely correcting their mistakes; however, special vigilance must be maintained against careerists, conspirators and double-dealers, so as to prevent such bad elements from usurping the leadership of the Party and the state at any level . . .". Many of these provisions concerning the duties of Party members were not referred to in the former Party Constitution, adopted in 1956, and were clearly a result of the Cultural Revolution.

Little is known of the social origins and occupational distribution of membership. In 1949, between 80 per cent and 90 per cent of the Party were from the peasantry, although by dint of strenuous efforts in the cities this had been reduced to under 70 per cent by 1957, at which time approximately 14 per cent were from the working class, with a similar percentage being classed as intellectuals, a group encompassing anyone having some form of higher education. The occupational distribution in 1956 showed some 60 per cent working in agriculture, 10 per cent in industry, 10 per cent as full-time employees of the Party apparatus, and 10 per cent in the armed forces with the remainder scattered in education and other areas. In terms of sex distribution, only 10 per cent are female, and even this low figure drops as soon as the higher levels of the Party are approached.

Cadres[3]

The ideology of the Party, the Thought of Mao Tse-tung, legitimises the Party's rule over state and society. By means of its cadres and tightly knit élite organisation and control over all other institutions, the Party mobilises society to achieve Party determined goals.

Cadres are the backbone of all leadership within communist China, ensuring the correct implementation of Party policy. In general, they are the individuals, who may or may not be Party members, who hold positions of leadership within the Party, state, army, communes or any other organisation. Within the Party, all cadres will be Party members, as will many, though by no means all cadres working in the governmental structure. Within the Party apparatus, Liu Shao-ch'i has said that "the leading bodies of the Party at all levels are composed of cadres. The cadres of the Party are the nucleus of the Party organisation and of the Chinese revolution".

In 1952 it was estimated that there were 2¾ million cadres (excluding military cadres) in the country, which rose to approximately six million cadres of all kinds by 1960.

Within the ranks of the Party cadres, seniority and authority depend primarily on the date of joining the Party, with precedence given to those who participated in the struggles in the Kiangsi soviet, or took part in the Long March. Following them come those cadres who were active in the Party during the war against the Japanese or in the civil war with the KMT. At the bottom of the hierarchy are those members who joined only after 1949.

Detailed files are maintained on the behaviour and political activities and attitudes of all cadres, who are expected to play an active role in regular "study sessions" where policy documents and ideological texts are read and discussed, and where all cadres may undergo criticism by their colleagues if it is felt that they are performing poorly in their work.

---

[3] Much of the following commentary on organisation describes the Party as it functioned prior to the changes wrought by the Cultural Revolution. The immediate effects of the Cultural Revolution are discussed later in the chapter. It is as yet too early to tell to what extent the revived Party will approximate its previous structure and function.

Although both Party and non-Party cadres attend the "study sessions," the separate identity of the Party élite is maintained by the existence of closed Party meetings, from which non-Party cadres are excluded. During Party meetings members will have access to documents and information denied to non-Party cadres, the secrecy of which maintains the division between the two groups.

Democratic centralism

Democratic centralism is "the organisational principle of the Party", states the new Party Constitution. The democratic aspects of this concept are first of all the election of leading Party organs at all levels. This refers to the election of Party committees by the Party congresses at each level in the hierarchy. At the highest level, the Central Committee is elected by the National Party Congress. The elected Party committees, which are executive bodies, are required to make work reports to their respective congresses at specified intervals, and "constantly listen to the opinions of the masses both inside and outside the Party, and accept their supervision".

Furthermore, although the centralist aspects of democratic centralism demand that "the individual is subordinate to the organisation, the minority is subordinate to the majority, the lower level is subordinate to the higher level, and the entire Party is subordinate to the Central Committee", nevertheless individual Party members are given the right, should they disagree with a Party decision or directive, to reserve their opinions, and report the difference of opinion direct to the Central Committee, bypassing other levels. Implementation of these new constitutional rights would make the Party more democratic than it was on the basis of the old 1956 Constitution. In practice, however, the centralist aspects of Party organisation tend to outweigh the democratic, and Party committees have the power to arrange their own re-election, so that the Party forms a pyramid with orders being transmitted from the apex down to the lowest levels for execution, and information concerning how policy is being implemented sent back up the Party chain of command.

The theory of democratic centralism was partially borrowed by the Chinese communists from the Russian Bolsheviks, and partially developed by them on the basis of their experiences in Yenan. Mao Tse-tung, believing in the all-pervasive existence of contradictions in the world, divided these contradictions into two types—antagonistic and non-antagonistic. The antagonistic contradictions, such as those between the CCP and the KMT, states Mao, can only be resolved by force. But non-antagonistic contradictions can exist even in socialist society, and they must be resolved, not by force, but by discussion and education. The contradiction between the interests of the individual and the interests of the state is an example of a non-antagonistic contradiction. Only the Party can correctly resolve these contradictions, for only the Party can perceive the "true" interests of the Chinese people.

In the case of the Party itself, the major contradiction is that between leaders and led. The Party requires that Party members unquestioningly obey directives from higher Party authorities, but obey them, not in the spirit of blind obedience, but with creativity and imagination. This was particularly vital during the Yenan period and the war against the Japanese, when it was necessary for all Party members to act in a unified manner as though under central control, although communication was poor among the scattered guerrilla base areas, and Party inspection of local areas was often impossible.

Democracy within the Party and the criticism of bureaucratic shortcomings results in cadres going out and explaining policy to the masses and winning their voluntary support, rather than acting "bureaucratically" and in a "commandist" manner, by sitting in their offices and issuing orders. Study sessions, criticism and self-criticism therefore help maintain organisational flexibility to suit local conditions, while strengthening the solidarity of Party members.

PARTY ORGANISATION AT THE NATIONAL LEVEL

The new Party Constitution, adopted by the Ninth Party Congress on 14 April 1969, is a much shorter and vaguer text than its predecessor adopted by the Eighth Party Congress of 1956. Although the description of the place, powers and functions of central Party organs do not, in general, conflict with those enumerated in the 1956 Constitution, the 1969 document describes them in far less detail, and the Party organisational structure has not yet been finally decided upon. (See Table 1.)

National Party Congress

The National Party Congress is the highest organ of the Party, and is constitutionally elected for a five-year term. In both the 1956 and 1969 Constitutions, there is a provision that "under special circumstances" the convening of the Party Congress may be advanced or delayed—by the Central Committee, according to the 1956 document, but unstated in 1969. It is supposed to meet in annual session (1956) but no frequency of meetings is specified in the new Constitution. According to both Constitutions the National Party Congress

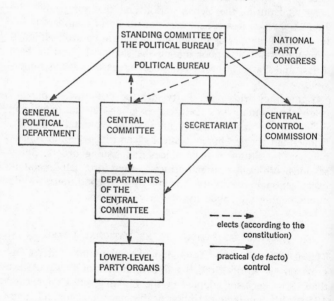

PARTY ORGANIZATION AT NATIONAL LEVEL
(ACCORDING TO 1956 CONSTITUTION)

TABLE 1

elects the Central Committee. It is also the body which hears and examines the reports of the Central Committee, determines the Party line and policy, and revises the Party Constitution, although none of these powers is mentioned in the 1969 version.

Nine Congresses have been held by the CCP from the founding Congress of 1921 to the most recent in 1969. There was a gap of eleven years between the Seventh Party Congress (1945) and the Eighth, and one of thirteen between the Eighth and Ninth Congresses. Far from convening in annual session, the Eighth Congress met only once more after 1956, at its second session in 1958. The Constitution is therefore by no means strictly adhered to.

Elections to the National Party Congress were similar in 1956 to the elections to the National People's Congress, being an indirect system of delegate conferences up the various rungs of the administrative ladder. Unlike the Constitution of the People's Republic, however, the electoral procedure was not referred to in any detail in the 1956 Party Constitution, which only noted that the number of delegates and the manner of their election was the responsibility of the Central Committee. The 1969 Constitution is even vaguer, saying only that "leading bodies of the Party at all levels are elected through democratic consultation", with no specific role assigned to the Central Committee.

Despite the constitutional provisions, the National Party Congress is not a body with any great power or authority. It meets but rarely, and then for only a few days, its membership is too large for proper discussion of major issues, and all the main decisions on policy are usually determined beforehand. The Ninth Party Congress appears to have been an exception to this generalisation. In September 1956 at the Eighth Congress, more than 1,000 delegates were present from the provinces, autonomous regions, the army, the cities and the government. They saw Mao open the Congress, and heard reports on the economy and the new Constitution by other Party leaders. All the major resolutions of the Congress had been determined in advance by a plenary session of the Central Committee.

However, the Congresses are vehicles for whipping up the

enthusiasm of Party members, and for bringing a section of the membership into direct contact with the leaders. The Party directs its sights towards new targets, and the Congresses may mark major changes in policy, as with the second session of the Eighth Congress held in May 1958, at the time of the Great Leap Forward, and the Ninth Congress witnessing the resuscitation of the Party following the Cultural Revolution.

Central Committee

According to the 1956 constitution, the Central Committee of the CCP has a wide range of responsibilities. It is elected by the National Party Congress for a five-year term, and is required to meet in plenary session at least twice per annum. It is responsible for convening the yearly sessions of the Party Congress, and is in charge of directing Party work while the Congress is not in session. It guides the work of central state organs and people's organisations through leading Party members' groups in them, instructs the People's Liberation Army through its control of the General Political Department, and elects the Politburo, the Secretariat, and the Chairman, Vice-Chairmen and General Secretary of the CCP.

The 1969 constitution refers but briefly to the fact that the Central Committee is elected by the National Party Congress, and that the Central Committee in turn elects the Politburo, the Standing Committee of the Politburo and the Chairman and Vice-Chairman of the Central Committee. The Secretariat and General Secretary are never specifically mentioned in the 1969 constitution. In line with the greater emphasis towards democracy in the new constitution, the Central Committee, as a leading Party organ, is required to hear the views of the masses both inside and *outside* the Party.

In terms of size, the Central Committee (CC) was expanded to 97 full and 73 alternate members by the Eighth Congress of 1956. Alternate members attend CC plenums, and have the right to speak but not vote. Vacancies on the CC are generally filled from among the alternates in order of precedence.

At the time of the second session of the Eighth Party Congress in 1958, two alternates were raised to full CC membership to fill vacancies caused by death, and 25 new alternates were created, making the total 97 full and 96 alternate members. The membership, formally elected by the Congress, was actually decided by discussion between the leaders of the delegate groups (in the case of the 1956 Congress) and Party leaders, with the delegates taking the "advice" of the outgoing Politburo and Central Committee.

Nor have the Central Committee plenums followed the twice per annum sessions ascribed to them by the 1956 constitution. Indeed, between the 1950 and 1954 plenums, there were no meetings at all, in spite of the fact that this period saw the Korean War and a large number of important domestic transformations such as land reform and the suppression of counter-revolutionaries. In recent years, the Ninth CC plenum was convened in January 1961, the Tenth in September 1962, the Eleventh in August 1966, and the Twelfth (and last plenum prior to the Ninth Party Congress) in October 1968. At these plenums, in addition to attendance by full and alternate CC members (those who were still active in the cases of the Eleventh and Twelfth plenums) other interested personnel may be asked to attend and take part in discussion, such as members of the departments under the CC, or members of provincial Party committees. Only full CC members have the right to vote, however. These provisions were swept aside (at least temporarily) during the Cultural Revolution. The Eleventh plenum was packed with Red Guards, who, although not allowed to vote, exercised an intimidating influence on the older personnel. Furthermore the Twelfth "enlarged" plenum of October 1968, which formally denounced Liu Shao-ch'i and sacked him from his Party and government posts, was hand-picked by Mao, with non-members being given full voting rights.

The role of the Central Committee is primarily to ratify the decisions taken by the Politburo and its Standing Committee. Rather than being a policy-making organ, it is more an organ which considers the proper implementation of policy. Its membership is important for the variety of major posts that they hold elsewhere in government and society. The élite making up the Central Committee are a well-educated group, most of them having experienced some kind of advanced education, often abroad. Rather than stemming from any kind of rural or urban proletariat, they tend to have middle-class backgrounds, being the sons of rich peasants or landlords. A high percentage of them come from the areas of Central and Central–South China, reflecting Party recruitment there in the early years of its history. Of the up-and-coming young men, a growing number are from North China. At least up until the time of the Cultural Revolution, the Party élite had manifested a unity and continuity which was quite remarkable by comparison with the leadership of other communist regimes.

Under the Central Committee are set up a number of working departments, each supervising a broad functional policy field, for example Organisation, Education, International Liaison, United Front, Propaganda, etc. In each case, work comes to the various departments of the CC from the Politburo via the Secretariat, which acts as a coordinating body and channels the work to the relevant department. The CC Organisation Department, for example, is responsible for the administration of all Party personnel, including their recruitment, postings, and training. In addition to the various departments, there are also a number of committees under the CC for Military Affairs, Women's Work, Social Affairs, etc. Most departments and committees will be headed by a member of the Central Committee.

Politburo and Standing Committee of the Politburo

According to the former Party Constitution, the Politburo and its Standing Committee are elected by a plenary session of the Central Committee, and exercise the powers and functions of the Central Committee when the CC itself is not in session. They are the bodies responsible for convening the biannual meetings of the CC. The Politburo and its Standing Committee are also responsible for directing the Secretariat. The Chairman and Vice-Chairmen of the CC hold the same posts with respect to the Politburo.

The new Constitution follows this pattern, but does not state the frequency with which CC plenums are convened by the Politburo, and omits all direct reference to the Secretariat.

The Politburo and its Standing Committee form the apex of the Party pyramid and are the key decision-making organs for all major policies within the state. This was the case up to the time of the Cultural Revolution, when the Politburo suffered a diminution of its power, the details of which are discussed later. Policy decisions flowed from the Politburo through the Secretariat, which acted as a clearing-house and channelled the commands to the appropriate department of the Central Committee for execution. It was the Politburo that directed the government, Party, army and all other organs of state and society, with top state institutions such as the National People's Congress giving an aura of legitimacy to policies predetermined by the Party. Prior to the Cultural Revolution, the Politburo probably met frequently, perhaps once a week or more, although its meetings were seldom announced, and then only after they had occurred.

In terms of size, the Politburo was enlarged at the Eighth Party Congress of 1956 from 13 full members to 17 full and 6 alternates. At the same time, a new body, the Standing Committee of the Politburo, was created, as a kind of "inner cabinet" of the enlarged Politburo, to be composed of the Chairman of the CC (Mao Tse-tung), the four Vice-Chairmen (Liu Shao-ch'i, Chou En-lai, Chu Teh and Ch'en Yün), and the General Secretary (Teng Hsiao-p'ing). The establishment of the posts of Vice-Chairmen of the CC was also an innovation of the Eighth Congress.

At the Fifth Plenum of the CC in May 1958, Lin Piao was made a Vice-Chairman of the CC, and elevated to the Standing Committee of the Politburo. Simultaneously, three new Politburo members were elected, making 20 full and 6 alternates, with 7 men on the Standing Committee.

The Politburo was somewhat depleted in membership in later years, with P'eng Teh-huai, Ch'en Yün and Chang Wen-t'ien suspended from active membership, three others dying, and P'eng Chen and Lu Ting-yi removed during the Cultural Revolution. Ch'en Yün was later rehabilitated to full membership, and the Politburo itself was returned to its former size by the Eleventh Plenum of the CC in August 1966, with the addition of many military figures. But reprieve was short-lived and the vicissitudes of the Cultural Revolution continued to shrink both the powers and membership of the Politburo and its Standing Committee. An example of the downgrading of the Politburo was the official Peking communiqué of January 1969, speaking of "Chairman Mao and Vice-Chairman Lin Piao receiving over 40,000 revolutionary fighters", in which twelve men were listed at the head of the article as "accompanying Chairman Mao", while members of the Politburo were listed well down in the article as only being "present on the occasion". However, the Politburo regained at least some of its former stature following the Ninth Congress.

Secretariat

Under the 1956 constitution the Secretariat was a key institution at the highest levels of the Party, "attending to the daily work of the Central Committee under the direction of the Politburo and its Standing Committee". The fact that the Secretariat became a focus of opposition to Mao Tse-tung led to its downgrading as an institution, and to the purging of much of its membership during the Cultural Revolution. Reflecting this, the 1969 Party constitution nowhere makes direct reference to the existence of the Secretariat, although article nine makes provision for its re-establishment, by stating that "under the leadership of the Chairman, Vice-Chairman and the Standing Committee of the Political Bureau of the Central Committee, a number of necessary organs, which are compact and efficient, shall be set up to attend to the day-to-day work of the Party, the government and the army in a centralised way".

Prior to the Cultural Revolution, the Secretariat was responsible for coordinating the work of the Politburo and its Standing Committee by referring their policy decisions to the relevant functional departments and committees under the Central Committee. Because of its routine control over these organs, the Secretariat had considerable real influence on policy, although not itself formally a policy-making organ. All of the members of the Secretariat (10 full and 7 alternates) were also members of the Central Committee, and 7 of them were on the Politburo. However, many of the most prominent victims of the Cultural Revolution purge were on the Secretariat, including Lu Ting-yi, Lo Jui-ch'ing, P'eng Chen, and the General Secretary, Teng Hsiao-p'ing. If the

Party is fully resuscitated after the Ninth Congress, there will have to be some organ to carry out its functions, whether or not the new body is called the Secretariat.

Other organs established at the central levels of the Party include the Central Control Commission and the General Political Department of the People's Liberation Army, both of which will be dealt with in later chapters.

Local Party organisation

The Party is organised like a pyramid. From its apex in the central Party organs it spreads out on a geographical and industrial basis through the regions, provinces, special districts, counties and districts to the basic level units set up in communes, factories, enterprises, offices, schools, streets and PLA units, in fact in every organisation where there are three or more Party members. The Party organisation parallels the state organisation at every level, so that in addition to the above-mentioned geographical divisions, Party organs will also be found in the corresponding autonomous regions and areas, and in the cities and towns. (See Table 2.)

The 1956 constitution did not accurately reflect Party organisation in its discussion of Party structure. For example, it made no reference to the existence of Party organisation at the special district and district levels, where they act as intermediate links in the chain of command, although not having elected Congresses as in the regular Party hierarchy. The constitution also referred to Party *hsiang* units, although with the communisation of 1958, the communes tended to merge with and replace the district, with the *hsiang* being transformed into the production brigade level. However, the failure of the Great Leap Forward, and the resulting shrinkage in size of the communes led to the re-emergence of the district, with the commune now merging with the *hsiang*.

At the Ninth Plenum of the Central Committee of January 1961, it was decided to re-create the six regional bureaux of the CC (North-east, North-west, North, Central-south, East and South-west) "to act for the CC in strengthening leadership over the Party committees in the various provinces, municipalities and autonomous regions". These regional bureaux were a recrudescence of the former Great Administrative

LOCAL ORGANIZATIONS OF THE
CHINESE COMMUNIST PARTY

CENTRAL LEVELS
|
REGIONAL BUREAUX OF
·THE CENTRAL COMMITTEE
|
PROVINCE
|
(SPECIAL DISTRICT)*
|
COUNTY
|
(DISTRICT)*
|
BASIC LEVEL
ORGANS

*THESE LEVELS ARE SET UP BY THE LEVEL ABOVE THEM,
FOR ADMINISTRATIVE CONVENIENCE

TABLE 2

Areas which were abolished in 1954. Unlike their earlier
counterparts, however, there were no corresponding parallel
government organisations at that level.

Each administrative level elects a Party congress, except for
the regional bureaux of the Central Committee, and the special district and district levels, which are purely agencies of
higher Party organs. Party Congresses are therefore held only
at the provincial and county levels (as well as nationally),
and in their corresponding autonomous and municipal units.

According to the 1956 Party constitution, the Party Congresses were elected for varying terms, ranging from three
years for a province to two for a county. The procedure for
the election of delegates to local Party Congresses and the
total number of delegates to be elected was determined by
the local Party committee, which was also responsible for convening the Congress. (Once per year for both provincial and

county levels.) In accordance with communist custom, the Congresses met infrequently, and then only for brief periods of time, so that real power was in the hands of the Party committees. Membership of the Party committees, and the Standing Committees and Secretariats elected by them, had to be approved by the Party committee on the next higher level. The 1969 constitution goes into far less detail concerning local Party organisation than its predecessor, specifying only that local Party Congresses elect their respective committees, and that "at the county level and upwards", Congresses are to be convened once every three years, although "under special circumstances, they may be convened before their due date or postponed".

Basic-level units

Basic-level units, or primary Party organisations, are established in every commune, village, enterprise, factory, school, office, street and PLA unit where there are three or more Party members. The members meet as a general branch meeting. Where the membership is large, a committee may be established. They must carry out the decisions of higher Party organs, and are responsible for executing propaganda and organisation work in their respective units, passing on the reactions of the people up the Party chain of command, raising the political and ideological level of the masses, recruiting new Party members and maintaining the discipline of Party members. Their most important function however is to "guide and supervise the administrative bodies and mass organisations in their respective units in the energetic fulfilment of the decisions of higher Party organisations and higher state organs". Although the 1969 constitution broadly outlines these functions for basic-level organisations, their prime task is stated as being "to lead the Party members and the broad revolutionary masses in studying and applying Marxism–Leninism–Mao Tsetung Thought in a living way".

The system in action

The Party's control over all aspects of life in China was explicitly described in its 1956 constitution. "The Party is the highest form of class organisation, and must strive to play a correct role as the leader and core in every aspect of the country's life . . . the Party plays the leading role in the life of the state and society." Again, the 1969 constitution reiterates this theme, by stating that "the Communist Party of China with Comrade Mao Tsetung as its leader is a great, glorious and correct Party and is the core of leadership of the Chinese people".

The Party is highly centralised, with commands flowing down from the Politburo or its Standing Committee through the Secretariat, via one of the departments of the Central Committee, and then down the local Party committees (or, more specifically, the various departments of these committees) to the basic level organs. The Party committees at every level are responsible for ensuring that all local work is correctly carried out, and that the government organs and people's organisations on their levels obey Party directives.

The Party apparatus parallels the government bureaucracy and exercises hegemony over it. Government organs at all levels, such as the People's Councils, correspond to the local Party committees, with the Party as the dominant organ. At the highest tier of the bureaucratic chain of command the departments of the Central Committee parallel the various offices of the State Council, each supervising a broad functional area of policy. Within the government organs, Party members will occupy the key leadership posts, and all the Party members in an organisation will form a Party branch to ensure that Party policy is correctly executed. However, in the case of government organs at the level of the county and above, the task of guidance within the organ is entrusted, not to the Party branch (the basic-level unit), but to the Party fraction, a group made up of the leading Party members in the branch. The tasks of the branch in these cases are restricted to the political and ideological supervision of branch members. In the case of one government ministry, for example, whereas the Party branch was composed of over 300 members, the fraction was made up of five men, and it was the fraction that was charged with ensuring Party authority within the ministry, and which in effect controlled the Party branch.[4] A Party fraction therefore, "when it is necessary to carry out its tasks, may place the Party branch in the same establishment under its direction and mobilise the entire Party membership in the establishment to aid in its work".[5]

Party authority within government organs is also buttressed by the presence within them of Party-controlled subsidiary organisations such as the Young Communist League and the trades unions. Members of the Young Communist League are directly subordinate to Party authority through the League organisation, and the trade union leadership is also Party-dominated, so that these organisations function as "transmission belts" between the Party and the non-Party masses and between the Party and non-Party cadres. Party control over government is also reinforced by Party control over the key Personnel Units within government organs. Leading positions in these units are invariably filled only by Party members, and since these units exercise command over the postings and careers of all civil servants (Party and non-Party), they "act as extensions into the government structure of the Party's organisation departments".[6]

It should be emphasised, however, that the Party does not consider that it has the function of carrying out the routine work of government. The Party sees itself as a directing organ, providing leadership and guidance, but not carrying out the day-to-day work. Often, however, particularly at the lower levels, the Party finds that the best way of getting the work done is to do it itself, and this provides a constant problem of demarcation for the Party leadership.

Young Communist League

With young people under twenty-five constituting as much as 60 per cent of the present Chinese population, and with the concern of the Chinese leadership about the future generation and the ability of these "heirs and successors" to carry the revolution forward, the CCP has always given a high

[4] A. Doak Barnett, *Cadres, Bureaucracy and Political Power in Communist China* (New York: Columbia University Press, 1967), p. 24.

[5] Liu Shao-ch'i, *On the Party* (Peking: Foreign Languages Press, 1952), p. 126.

[6] Barnett, op. cit., p. 20.

priority to the organisation of youth, to ensure that they adopt the correct attitudes and political standpoint. The first communist youth organisation, the Socialist Youth League, with its foundation in 1920, in fact antedated the creation of the Party itself. This body went through many changes of name, and finally adopted its current title of Young Communist League (YCL) only in May 1957.

The YCL, while accepting the leadership of its parent organ, is organisationally independent, having its own hierarchy from national to local levels, paralleling the Party organs, with YCL committees at each level responsible to both the Party committee on the same level, and the YCL committee on the next higher level.

The YCL functions as one of the most important CCP "transmission belts" for carrying the influence of the Party into the schools, student associations, and other areas of society. It is an organisational arm of the Party, helping the Party particularly in its propaganda work, and guaranteeing the adoption of correct attitudes towards the Party and its work by young people.

Membership of the YCL is open to those aged fifteen to twenty-five. Those who become full CCP members must quit the YCL, unless they hold a leading position within the organisation, in which case they may remain YCL members until aged twenty-eight. Most new CCP members are recruited from the YCL, although not all YCL members can expect to join the Party. From a total of half a million in 1949, the YCL had expanded to twenty-five million by 1959. This rapid growth brought problems in its train, such as a decline in political standards. From 1959 on, recruitment stagnated, and the membership aged, a substantial minority being over twenty-five, and many of the leading posts filled by those over the legal age limit of twenty-eight.

In an attempt to counter this decline, the YCL launched a major recruiting campaign in 1965 that brought in a vast influx of 8½ million new members. However, the relaxation of admission requirements necessary to recruit so many led inevitably to a decline of standards. Partially because of its links with those who opposed Mao's leadership, the YCL became a casualty of the Cultural Revolution, and with the advent of the Red Guards in the summer of 1966, the YCL ceased to function, and its journals ceased publication. Given the necessity to organise youth in some way on the part of the CCP leaders, it is likely that with the passing of the Red Guards from the scene, the YCL will be resurrected in some form. The 1969 Party constitution did refer to the acceptance of Party Leadership by the YCL, and it was announced in July 1969 that "work on the consolidation of the Communist Youth League should also begin".

Young Pioneers

The Young Pioneers are under the leadership of the YCL and have no separate organisation of their own. Open to children aged nine to fifteen, they were formed in 1949, and had approximately 50 million members in 1962. Organised particularly in the schools, it is estimated that between 35 per cent and 40 per cent of all primary-school children were Young Pioneers. Like the YCL, their prime function was to indoctrinate children with the correct Party attitudes, and the YCL drew many of its recruits from the Young Pioneers. Like the YCL, the Young Pioneers have faded from the scene with the advent of the Cultural Revolution.

New youth organs

New "Children's Leagues" and "Juvenile Leagues" were initially referred to by a plenum of the YCL Central Committee of May 1965. It was never clear as to whether they would be complementary or replacement organs for the YCL and the Young Pioneers, and they never got beyond the experimental state. During the Cultural Revolution, mention was made of "Little Red Soldiers" and the "League of Red Children", apparently hearkening back to similar communist children's groups of the 1930s, but little of substance has been heard of them.

Rectification campaigns

A rectification campaign is "an ideological remoulding campaign conducted throughout the Party aimed at exposing and rectifying all incorrect tendencies and practices displayed by

Party members in various fields of work".[7] Liu Shao-ch'i was here speaking of the *cheng-feng* movement of 1941–2, but the description fits the periodic campaigns that have swept over China since 1949. All the campaigns are directed against specific abuses, generally attributed to bureaucratic practices of some kind, and are designed to improve the work of the Party, tighten up Party discipline, eliminate or reform lax members, and raise ideological standards.

Rectification campaigns are often linked to some particular Party policy, such as the land reform movement of 1950, so that basic level Party units might better execute major policy. Party committees at all levels meet with increasing frequency, studying selected texts of Mao Tse-tung, Marx, Lenin or current policy documents. All Party members are expected and encouraged to indulge in criticism of their own, and others', shortcomings, and certain cadres will be selected as negative examples, not to be followed. These periodic campaigns, and the omni-present threat of campaigns to come, keep Party members in a perpetual state of tension. Combined with the study sessions are the Party committees' reassessment of personnel under their command, together with a re-evaluation of their past background in the light of information culled from the Party's personnel files. Cadres found to be delinquent in work or behaviour may be demoted, transferred or sentenced to reform through labour.

The first major campaign of this kind was the *cheng-feng*, or rectification movement of 1941–2 (see Chapter 1). The second was carried out in the "liberated areas" in 1947–8, and was aimed at the smooth execution of the land reform policy. The campaign of 1950–3, the first since liberation, screened the vast influx of new blood that had joined the Party after 1949, many of whom were careerists jumping on the bandwagon. Clearly, political standards needed raising, and even some of the old cadres had taken too easily to the comforts of the cities. The Party also placed strong stress, now that it had gained nation-wide victory, on winning over the majority of the non-Party masses to their side.

Several other campaigns of the same period were directed

[7] Liu Shao-ch'i, op. cit., p. 190.

at suppressing counter-revolutionaries, and opposing waste and corruption within the Party.

The disgrace and purge in 1954 of Kao Kang and Jao Shu-shih, bosses of the North-east (Manchuria) and East China Great Administrative Areas respectively, was followed by a movement within the Party to strengthen local ties with Peking.

The gradual liberalisation of Party policy towards the intellectuals in 1956 and early 1957, culminating in the brief "100 flowers" period of May–June 1957 (during which time strong criticism was made by the intellectuals of the Party) led to a reimposition of Party discipline in June, and the anti-rightist campaign of 1957–8, aimed at all those within and without the Party who had joined in the criticism (see Chapter 5).

A later example of the rectification campaigns was the Socialist Education Movement of 1962–6, launched in the aftermath of the failure of the Great Leap, and designed to rectify shortcomings of cadres at the basic levels of the Party and to improve Party work at the grass roots. Corruption among cadres was increasing, and the tendency for the peasant to concentrate his efforts on his own private plot was spreading. The campaign was aimed at counteracting these "insidious" influences, and to inculcate the virtues of thrift and self-reliance among the population. In its later stages, the Socialist Education Movement became linked to policy differences at the highest levels of the Party, and became a prelude to the largest and most widespread rectification campaign of them all—the Cultural Revolution.

The Great Proletarian Cultural Revolution

By the early 1960s, Mao was becoming increasingly concerned about the spectre of "revisionism" that he saw haunting China. The question in his mind was one of how to ensure the continuity of the revolution after his own death, by instilling in the minds of youth, the "heirs and successors" of the revolution, the ideals and purpose of the hallowed days on Chingkangshan and in the caves of Yenan—days which the rising generation had never shared. The problem that Mao faced, therefore, was how to continue with the modernisation of the country without letting economic development, and the growth of routinisation and bureaucratisation lead to any decline in ideological fervour.

Mao did not have to look far for concrete manifestations of his fears that revisionism was developing. The early 1960s, which followed the disasters of the Great Leap Forward, bad harvests, and the withdrawal of Soviet aid and technicians, had resulted in many Party personnel questioning the validity of the Maoist strategy of economic and political development. In addition, the economic crisis had led to some liberalisation, caused by the need to make use of the technical and managerial skills of the intellectuals, and to greater freedom in the economic sphere in the form of economic decentralisation and greater personal incentives. These developments led to a certain recrudescence of private enterprise on a small scale. However, as soon as the economy showed signs of improvement, Mao launched a counter-attack against these pernicious tendencies, by means of the Socialist Education Movement which began following the Tenth Plenum of the CC in the autumn of 1962.

The Socialist Education Movement was a forerunner of the Cultural Revolution, and was designed to combat the "unhealthy tendencies" (such as the growth in importance of the peasants' private plots and the fall in cadre morale) that had arisen during the 1959–62 period. The movement involved the sending-down of many CCP cadres from the city to the countryside to live and work with the peasants on the communes, greater reliance being placed on the poor and lower-middle peasants by giving them more posts of responsibility, the emulation of the PLA as a model to follow, and increased study of the Thoughts of Mao Tse-tung. By 1966, the Socialist Education Movement had merged with the mainstream of the Cultural Revolution.

By the mid-1960s, Mao felt that his policies for permanent revolutionary change were meeting with opposition from persons at the very highest level of the Party apparatus, and were also suffering from the sheer inertia of the Party bureaucracy. The Cultural Revolution was an attempt to overcome this dilemma. In all probability, the escalation of the Vietnam War in the summer of 1965, with the arrival of increased

numbers of US troops at that time, was a contributing factor
in the initial stages of the Cultural Revolution. The deployment of so many new "imperialist" troops close to China's
borders brought about a debate within the PLA between the
"professionals", who favoured a modern army equipped with
the most advanced technology, and less use of the military
for economic purposes, and the advocates of defensive guerrilla warfare, the two sides being personified by Lo Jui-ch'ing
(Chief of Staff) and Lin Piao (Minister of Defence). The
Maoist viewpoint of Lin Piao was victorious, and Lin published his victory paean "Long Live the Victory of People's
War" later that year. Lo Jui-ch'ing ceased to appear in any
official capacity after November 1965. Mao came more and
more to feel that he could rely on the army, and use it as a
model of revolutionary purity for the Party to emulate, particularly since the PLA was under the command of such a
firm supporter as Lin Piao.

The first stage of the Cultural Revolution was launched
by Mao at a working conference of the Central Committee
in September 1965. At that time, a group of five high Party
officials were formed into a Cultural Revolution Group, led
by P'eng Chen, Politburo member and Mayor of Peking. At
the same time, Mao chose three bases for his attack against
the Chinese intellectuals and the Party propaganda apparatus,
which Mao thought were responsible for the spread of revisionist ideas. In addition to the PLA, Mao chose to base his
strategy on the Shanghai Party apparatus, and on the theoretical journal *Red Flag,* edited by Ch'en Po-ta, his former secretary, and a loyal follower.

The first salvo came in November 1965 when a Shanghai
paper attacked Wu Han, the non-communist deputy mayor of
Peking, for his Peking opera *Hai Jui Dismissed from Office,*
performed in 1961. This was held to be an allegorical attempt to criticise Mao for his unjust sacking of P'eng Teh-
huai in 1959. Since Wu Han was deputy mayor under P'eng
Chen, this criticism naturally led to conflict between Mao
and P'eng himself, particularly since the latter, as head of the
Cultural Revolution Group, had done his best to protect the
propaganda organs and restrict the purge to one of criticism
and discussion only. After a struggle lasting for some months

(Mao later claimed that "you could not drive a pin into the Peking Party apparatus"), Mao emerged victorious. P'eng made his last appearance in March 1966, and was replaced in June by Li Hsüeh-feng, head of the Central Committee's North China Bureau. In addition to his position as head of the Peking Party Committee, P'eng was also the sixth ranking member of the Politburo, and second secretary of the Secretariat under Teng Hsiao-p'ing.

The pressure mounted in the spring of 1966 with further attacks on, and purges of, university presidents, university Party secretaries, teachers and other intellectuals, as well as the Party propaganda machine. A Politburo meeting in May confirmed the dismissal of P'eng Chen, and set up a new Cultural Revolution Group of eighteen directly under the Standing Committee of the Politburo and headed by Ch'en Po-ta. The only person to be carried over from the former group was K'ang Sheng. The new group also included T'ao Chu, first Secretary of the Central–South Bureau, and Chiang Ch'ing, Mao's wife.

In July, Lu Ting-yi, the head of the Party's Propaganda Department, fell from grace, as did his deputy Chou Yang. Lu's post was filled by T'ao Chu, who carried out a thorough purge of the propaganda machine ostensibly to make it more responsive to Mao's ideas.

Neither Liu Shao-ch'i nor Teng Hsiao-p'ing supported what appeared to them to be an indiscriminate dismantling of the machine which they had laboured to perfect over so many decades. While Mao was absent from Peking in June, they sent work teams to various universities and Party organisations in order to "guide" the Cultural Revolution. The work teams were designed to ensure that the purge was kept within controlled limits, and did not damage the apparatus or top Party members, by keeping it carefully within the control of the Secretariat, rather than being run by the masses under orders from Mao and his Cultural Revolution Group. The work teams clashed with the teenage Red Guards (who had made their first appearance in May), and were withdrawn when Mao returned to Peking in July.

The Eleventh Plenum of the Central Committee held in August 1966 approved the progress of the Cultural Revolution, and laid down the guidelines for future events in the form of sixteen points. The plenum was illegally packed by Red Guards, and called upon Party committees at all levels to "put daring above everything else, boldly arouse the masses, change the state of weakness and incompetence where it exists . . . and dismiss from their leading posts all those in authority who are taking the capitalist road and so make possible the recapture of the leadership for the proletarian revolutionaries".[8]

Both Liu and Teng were in a weak position from this time on. Liu was demoted from second to eighth place in the hierarchy, and Lin Piao was made the Party's only Vice-Chairman, second in command to Mao Tse-tung. Teng's Secretariat had lost several men through the purge—P'eng Chen, Lo Jui-ch'ing, Lu Ting-yi and Yang Shang-k'un (head of the CC General Affairs office). New members of the Politburo were three in all—T'ao Chu (who fell into disgrace December 1966), Ch'en Po-ta and K'ang Sheng. But the most significant point of the plenum was the fact that the Party was dismissed as unsuitable for reforming itself, and this task was handed over to the PLA, and especially to the masses and the Red Guards.

The Red Guards made their first public appearance at a mass rally in Peking on 18 August. Although they attacked the CCP committees and Party members by means of big character posters, newspapers, and struggle meetings, the Party machine was successful in warding off their attacks for some months, by forming Red Guard teams of their own as a means of self-preservation. But in December 1966, the Cultural Revolution took on a new turn. The Red Guards, under orders from the Cultural Revolution Group controlled by Mao, and urged on by the propaganda machine now under Mao's command, were told to wreck the Party machine and replace it by a revolutionary seizure of power from below. Red Guards staged occupations of Party and government offices and arranged confrontations between officials and masses. After the fall of Li Hsüeh-feng (P'eng Chen's replacement as head of the Peking CCP Municipal Committee),

[8] Decision of the Central Committee of the CCP concerning the Great Proletarian Cultural Revolution. Adopted on 8 August 1966 (Point 3).

no new successor was announced and this, plus references to "the former Party committee" marked the dissolution of the Party apparatus.

The new power structure to replace the existing Party and government machinery was to be modelled on the Paris Commune of 1871, and the first "victory" took place in January 1967 in Shanghai.

The chaotic situation in Shanghai testified to the fact that although it was relatively simple to intimidate the Party and government cadres, and to dismantle the old administrative apparatus, it was less simple to replace it with anything else. Disruption spread across China as Red Guards elsewhere attempted to emulate the example of Shanghai, and industrial production fell as the Party apparatus fought back by staging fake seizures of power by its own ostensibly Maoist mass organisations, by sending workers off to Peking in search of higher wages, and by creating strikes.

Mao was forced to prevent the situation from degenerating further by calling on the PLA in January to take over the administrative structure so that government could continue to function, and secondly, by repudiating the Shanghai Paris Commune as a model to be copied. The PLA, which had had a somewhat passive role until this time, now intervened to restore law and order, and to stand in for the defunct Party and government provincial committees. Revolutionary seizures of power were now to take the form of Revolutionary Committees, which were triple alliances made up of the PLA, Red Guards and loyal (Maoist) cadres. Since the Red Guards frequently had difficulty deciding among themselves which of them was to be represented on the Revolutionary Committee, and since many cadres were unwilling to become targets of abuse yet again, power largely devolved on to the PLA as the only nation-wide organisation with its command structure still intact. The PLA maintained order in most provinces by the use of Military Control Commissions, since the "seizure of power" had only been successful (by the end of February 1967) in the city of Shanghai, and the provinces of Heilungkiang, Kweichow, Shansi and Shantung. As from this time, the PLA was directly concerned with the administration of the economy.

In March another "swing to the left" became apparent. The Red Guards, quarrelling among themselves, resented the new authority of the PLA and the re-emergence of the former cadres. Their discontent, exploited by Mao, led to clashes between the Red Guards and the PLA in the provinces, and attacks by the Red Guards on central government offices and officials in Peking. As spring moved into summer, armed clashes across the country grew, with the Red Guards looting and destroying as they fought among themselves and with the army for political advantage. With violence spreading, only one more Revolutionary Committee was established during that time—in Peking in April. To speed up the process, delegations were sent from Peking to quell the violence, and help provincial authorities form Revolutionary Committees. This climaxed with the Wuhan Incident of July–August when two high-ranking officials from Peking, Hsieh Fu-chih and Wang Li, were held under temporary arrest in a factional battle between two Red Guard units.

With chaos growing in the summer of 1967, and with the real danger that such traditionally independent provinces remote from Peking, such as Tibet, Sinkiang, Inner Mongolia and Szechuan might reassert their autonomy, Mao ordered a return to moderation, and sent in the army to restrain Red Guard factionalism by force of arms if necessary. Nevertheless, the setting up of Revolutionary Committees, supposed to be completed by January 1968, progressed at a slow pace. They were formed in the provinces of Chinghai (August) and Inner Mongolia (November), but the majority of the country was still without them, mainly due to the inability of the Red Guard groups to agree among themselves as to how they were to form their own representation on the triple alliances. This situation led to a new strategy by the end of the year—one of stressing the need to recruit former Party and government cadres, and rely on their administrative ability rather than the revolutionary ardour of immature youth. Attempts were made to get the Red Guards back into the classrooms with threats of failure to graduate.

Some former high officials, such as Ch'en Yi, Minister of Foreign Affairs, reappeared in their offices after being under criticism for over a year.

This trend towards moderation was also exemplified by the twelve Revolutionary Committees which were set up between January and April 1968, on which the moderates, namely the PLA and former cadres, were predominant, which contrasted with the Revolutionary Committees formed in the same months of 1967, on which the Red Guards had a far higher representation. Absenteeism and strikes in industry were condemned as sabotage, and the PLA took control over public security and rail communications. Some members of the Cultural Revolution Group, including Wang Li and Ch'i Pen-yü, were denounced as "ultra-leftists". Yet another resurgence of violence flared up again between May and July of 1968, possibly engineered by Mao's wife, Chiang Ch'ing, in an attempt to claim a greater representation on the Revolutionary Committees for the Red Guards and revolutionary rebels (workers). Certainly this stratagem was successful in the case of the three Committees set up in May in Liaoning, Shensi and Szechuan. Simultaneously, the PLA's acting Chief of Staff, Yang Ch'eng-wu, was dismissed, and other high-ranking government officials were subjected to a recurrence of attacks from big-character posters and the Red Guard press. Pitched battles broke out again as extreme Red Guards attacked their more moderate rivals. Trussed and headless bodies floated by the dozen into Hong Kong harbour, victims of the factional strife. With the loss of political stability, no Revolutionary Committees were set up in June or July, although the leaders of many provinces sent delegations to Peking to negotiate on their establishment. In July, Mao was once again forced to rely on the PLA and call on the armed forces to stop the escalating conflict. This last burst of fighting was to prove to be political death for the Red Guards.

In July, Mao charged that the students had let him down. Teams of workers and peasants, backed by the PLA were sent to schools and factories to restore order and get the economy on the move. With his symbolic gift of mangoes to the team working at Tsinghua University, Mao gave his seal of approval to their work, and at the same time signalled the downgrading of the Red Guards. On 5 September 1968 China became "all red", with the establishment of Revolutionary Committees in all twenty-six provinces and three centrally controlled cities (Peking, Shanghai and Tientsin).

At the Twelfth enlarged plenum of the Central Committee convened in October 1968, gone were the fanatical Red Guards, and in their places sat "responsible comrades from Revolutionary Committees of provinces, municipalities and autonomous regions", together with PLA members. The plenum sounded a distinctly conservative note by comparison with the previous Eleventh session. Liu Shao-ch'i was expelled from his positions, and from the Party, but surprisingly, no formal action was taken against his cohort Teng Hsiao-p'ing. The plenum also drafted the new Party constitution.

An increased political role for the military was an inevitable concomitant of the destruction of the Party apparatus, and the giving of the PLA such a commanding role in government and administration. This commanding role was reflected in the PLA representation on the provincial Revolutionary Committees. Designed to be triple alliances, it transpired that on the committees set up after early 1967, the local military had more than one-third of the committee positions. After the summer of 1967 the vast majority of chairmen and first vice-chairmen of the Revolutionary Committees were high-ranking military officers, so that the former Party and government apparatus had been replaced by a new regional military power structure.

The relationship between the military, the Revolutionary Committees, and the CCP following the Ninth Party Congress is not clear. There was increased emphasis on "Party building" at the time of the Congress in April 1969, and it would seem that Party cadres are to form the core of the new Revolutionary Committees, once the Party apparatus has been reconstructed on a nation-wide scale. According to an article in *Peking Review*[9] concerning a factory Revolutionary Committee, it was stated that the standing committee of the revolutionary committee was the same as the leading Party members' group in the plant. Of the twenty-four members of the Party's leading group, two were PLA representatives, fourteen were "new born forces" who had emerged during the

[9] *Peking Review*, no. 15 (11 April 1969), pp. 33–7.

Cultural Revolution, and three had been selected from among the plant's workers. Presumably the remaining five were old Party cadres. The article stated that "the new leading body exercises unified leadership organisationally. The standing committee (all are full Party members) of the revolutionary committee is the Party leading group and the political instructors of the companies (the workshops) are Party branch secretaries".[10] Since the Party now appears to dominate the organs of the Revolutionary Committees, the question of control becomes one of who controls the Party committees in the amalgam of PLA men, loyal Maoists who came to the fore during the Cultural Revolution, and former cadres.

In overview, it seems clear that there was no Maoist grand strategic plan for the unfolding of the Cultural Revolution. The fact that four out of five of the original Cultural Revolution Group were purged, as were a large number of the Group which succeeded it, argues against any detailed preconceived stratagem. Nor does it seem likely that Mao started the Cultural Revolution with the initial intention of destroying the Party apparatus, for otherwise neither Liu Shao-ch'i nor Teng Hsiao-p'ing would have been re-elected to the reorganised Standing Committee of the Politburo at the Eleventh CC plenum of August 1966. Chou En-lai later reported that they were not dismissed then because it was hoped that they would see the error of their ways.

The Cultural Revolution virtually destroyed the Communist Party, with its former members scattered and demoralised. Even though the Party will be resurrected, it is doubtful if it can ever regain the transcendental position it once held in Chinese society. Its claim to possess absolute political truth has been shattered, many of its most senior members disgraced or dismissed. By removing so many high- and middle-level cadres, however, a degree of upward mobility will have been created that was not present before, and had for a long time been a problem in the Party.

Another factor mitigating against a prearranged sequence of events on the part of Mao has been the ever-increasing involvement of the army in the political life of the country—

[10] *Peking Review,* op. cit., p. 36.

thus reversing the Maoist dictum that "the Party controls the gun, and will never allow the gun to command the Party". However, with the reformation of the Party apparatus, it is likely that the Party will gradually attempt to reassert itself, although it remains to be seen whether the military will be content to retreat to its former position of second fiddle.

The real heresy of Liu Shao-ch'i and Teng Hsiao-p'ing was not that they were actually agents of the bourgeoisie or of the Kuomintang trying to stage a "capitalist restoration", but that they possessed different views on the future of China's political and economic development to those held by Mao Tsetung. They apparently tried to restrain Mao at the time of the Great Leap Forward, to reinstate the disgraced P'eng Tehhuai (who had argued for a *rapprochement* with the Russians), and had tried to keep the Cultural Revolution within carefully demarcated boundaries, controlled by the Party itself.

Mao has won a temporary political victory, but whether his Yenan vision, with its emphasis on "guerrilla-ism", human will, the spiritual transformation of man, and of a life of perpetual struggle is as compatible with the realities of contemporary China as a modernising society as it was in the days of Chingkangshan, is open to serious doubt.

Ninth Party Congress

References to "Party construction" and to the Ninth Congress appeared at intervals during the Cultural Revolution from 1967 onwards, but preparations for the Congress only began in earnest after the CC plenum of October 1968. Unlike the 1956 Congress, to which delegates were elected from all registered Party members (a situation unique in the history of CCP Congresses), delegates to the Ninth Congress were selected from the top downwards by means of "mass consultation", which ensured that a degree of control over them was maintained by the leaders of the Cultural Revolution. Only eight provincial revolutionary committees were reported to have held meetings at which Congress delegates may have been selected. The length of time taken to organise the Congress was indicative of probable disagreement among the leaders as to what kind of new Communist Party was to rise from the ashes of the revolution. The more extremist among them, such as Yao Wen-yüan and Chang Ch'un-ch'iao, favoured a large intake of Red Guards and new "revolutionary" cadres into the Party, while other more moderate elements, like Hsieh Fu-chih, were disinclined to grant mass entry to large numbers of undisciplined students.

The Ninth Party Congress was the first new Congress for thirteen years. It was called to approve retroactively the events of the Cultural Revolution and to sanctify the purge which had eliminated much of the opposition to Mao within the Party leadership, to restore Party morale, to ratify a new Party constitution, and to build a revolutionised Party apparatus. The Congress opened on 1 April and closed on 24 April 1969. Unlike the Eighth Party Congress, few of the speeches were published, and few details issued concerning the proceedings. The number of delegates totalled 1,512 and after Mao had declared the Congress open, the agenda consisted of the Political Report to be given by Lin Piao, the ratification of the new Party constitution, and the election of a new Central Committee.

Lin Piao's Political Report, only published after the close of the Congress, looked to the "Thought of Mao Tse-tung" as the fount of all wisdom, and consisted largely of a recapitulation of the history of the Cultural Revolution and the crimes of Liu Shao-ch'i, followed by a shorter section of the role of the Party. This stressed the part played by the military, and indicated that the revolutionary committees might serve as the future core of a rejuvenated CCP. The Report concluded with an analysis of China's foreign relations, in which it was made clear that Peking now judged the Soviet Union, and not the United States, to be the chief enemy.

The new Party constitution was passed by the Congress on 14 April. Except for a few changes of minor detail, it did not differ from the draft constitution introduced to the Congress, and which has already been discussed.

There were 176 individuals who were initially elected to the temporary Presidium of the Congress, and who later formed the core of the new Central Committee. Only about 25 per cent of the Congress Presidium was made up of former full or alternate members of the 1958 Central Committee. The new CC was allegedly elected by secret ballot, though no doubt a strong element of central direction was also present. There was evidence of considerable disagreement at the Congress about the composition of the CC because it took no less than ten days to complete the election. The new CC totalled 279 in all, with 170 full members, and 109 alternates. Unlike previous CC listings, the names of the Ninth CC were listed (after Chairman Mao Tse-tung and Vice-Chairman Lin Piao who headed the list) in order of number of strokes to the Chinese characters making up their names (the Chinese equivalent of alphabetical order), rather than the previous method of listing by rank order of votes received on the ballot. Many of the military figures on the Congress Presidium found their way on to the CC, as in fact did all but thirty-five of the Presidium, those left off being primarily representatives of the masses such as "model workers". There were 141 "new" men (not on the Congress Presidium) who were elected to the CC.

Of the 170 man Eighth CC, only 52 were retained on the Ninth CC. The most significant thing about the new CC was the strength of the military representation, since they accounted for 123 or 44 per cent of the total, of whom 80 were officials of the Military Region and Military District commands, and 56 held appointments on the provincial Revolutionary Committees concurrently with a regional military post. All 29 Revolutionary Committee chairmen were on the CC, and most provinces had additional members on the CC as well. The commanders of all 13 Military Regions were members of the new CC. In addition, some 30 Ministers and other central government officials were represented on the new CC, together with two ambassadors (Huang Chen and Keng Piao), 15 workers, 16 peasants, the missile expert Ch'ien Hsüeh-sen (alternate member), cultural spokesman Kuo Mo-jo, historian Fan Wen-lan, and only two Red Guard leaders, Nieh Yüan-tzu from Peking University and Ch'en Kan-feng of Tungchi University in Shanghai (both as alternate members). The new CC also included some leaders heavily criticised during the Cultural Revolution, such as the former Party and military leader of Sinkiang, Wang En-mao (now Vice-Chairman of the Sinkiang Revolutionary Committee, and elected only as an alternate CC member), and Yü Ch'iu-li (Minister of Petroleum, elected as a full member).

At its first plenary session on 28 April the new CC elected the highest organs of the Party, the Politburo and the Standing Committee of the Politburo. To the Politburo were elected 25 individuals, 21 full members and four alternates. From among the full members, a Standing Committee of five, Mao Tse-tung, Lin Piao, Ch'en Po-ta, Chou En-lai and K'ang Sheng, was elected. The full members of the Politburo were Mao Tse-tung and Lin Piao (and by stroke order), Yeh Ch'ün, Yeh Chien-ying, Liu Po-ch'eng, Chiang Ch'ing, Chu Teh, Hsü Shih-yu, Ch'en Po-ta, Ch'en Hsi-lien, Li Hsien-nien, Li Tso-p'eng, Wu Fa-hsien, Chang Ch'un-ch'iao, Ch'iu Hui-tso, Chou En-lai, Yao Wen-yüan, K'ang Sheng, Huang Yung-sheng, Tung Pi-wu, and Hsieh Fu-chih. The four alternates were Chi Teng-k'uei, Li Hsüeh-feng, Li Teh-sheng and Wang Tung-hsing. In each case the listing followed the same pattern; Mao and Lin came first, and the rest followed in stroke order, as though to emphasise that Mao and his chosen successor lived on a different plane to the others. Shortly after the plenum, however, other official pronouncements made it clear that Chou En-lai was still no. 3 in order of precedence.

The Standing Committee of the Politburo was slightly reduced in size—formerly seven, now five. All of the five were Politburo members at least since 1958, and they had all been on the Standing Committee prior to 1969 (Mao and Chou En-lai since the creation of the Standing Committee in 1956, Lin since 1958, and Ch'en Po-ta and K'ang Sheng since 1967).

Of the 26 members of the 1966 Politburo (20 full and six alternates), 17 were not on the new body. Of these 17, three had died (K'o Ch'ing-shih, Lin Po-ch'ü and Lo Jung-huan); three survived politically to be on the new Central Committee but not on the Politburo (Ch'en Yi, Ch'en Yün and Li Fu-ch'un), and eleven were purged in the course of the Cultural Revolution, or by earlier events (full members Ho Lung, Li Ch'ing-ch'üan, Liu Shao-ch'i, P'eng Chen, P'eng Teh-huai,

T'an Chen-lin and Teng Hsiao-p'ing; and alternate members Chang Wen-t'ien, Lu Ting-yi, Po Yi-po and Ulanfu).

The nine former members who survived to be re-elected to the new Politburo were Ch'en Po-ta, Chou En-lai, Chu Teh, K'ang Sheng, Li Hsien-nien, Lin Piao, Liu Po-ch'eng, Mao Tse-tung and Tung Pi-wu. In addition, sixteen new members were added.

The composition of the new Politburo showed a heavy increase in military representation. If one includes Public Security officials together with active military officers, there were thirteen (over 50 per cent) who could be classed as "military men". These included three men who were on the old Politburo—Chu Teh, Lin Piao and Liu Po-ch'eng (all marshals), plus no fewer than ten newcomers to the office—Ch'en Hsi-lien (commander of the Shenyang [Mukden] Military Region and Chairman of the Liaoning Revolutionary Committee), Ch'iu Hui'tso (director of army logistics), Hsieh Fu-chih (Minister of Public Security and head of the Peking Revolutionary Committee), Hsü Shih-yu (commander of the Nanking Military Region and Chairman of the Kiangsu Revolutionary Committee), Huang Yung-sheng (Chief of Staff and Chairman of the Kwangtung Revolutionary Committee), Li Teh-sheng (military commander of Anhwei and Chairman of the Anhwei Revolutionary Committee), Li Tso-p'eng (Navy first political commissar), Wang Tung-hsing (Deputy Minister of Public Security and Mao's former body-guard), Wu Fa-hsien (Air Force commander) and Yeh Chien-ying (PLA marshal). Furthermore, it was announced in May 1969 that three former PLA marshals, Ch'en Yi, Hsü Hsiang-ch'ien and Nieh Jung-chen were appointed as Vice-Chairmen of the CC's Military Commission. All three are on the new CC, although Ch'en Yi was demoted from his former Politburo membership.

Of the twelve non-military members on the new Politburo, two were wives of members, Mao's wife Chiang Ch'ing, and Yeh Ch'ün, the wife of Lin Piao. Yeh Ch'ün made her first recorded public appearance only in December 1966, and was not identified as the wife of Lin Piao until January 1967. Chiang Ch'ing is Mao's fourth wife (they married in 1939) and emerged as a leader of the Cultural Revolution in the summer of 1966. Chiang Ch'ing was adviser to the Cultural Revolution Group, and Yeh Ch'ün was a member of the PLA's Cultural Revolution Group. Associated with them were former Cultural Revolution Group members Chang Ch'un-ch'iao, Ch'en Po-ta, K'ang Sheng and Yao Wen-yüan. In spite of being associates, this cannot be considered a cohesive group. K'ang is a shadowy figure who has worked as head of intelligence; Ch'en Po-ta is Mao's amanuensis; and Chang Ch'un-ch'iao and Yao Wen-yüan both rose rapidly up the political ladder as a result of the Cultural Revolution—Chang as a secretary of the former Shanghai Party Committee and of the East China Bureau, and Yao as a literary figure who fired the first shots in the Cultural Revolution with his article criticising Wu Han's play *Hai Jui Dismissed from Office*. Of the remainder, Chi Teng-k'uei is a Vice-Chairman of the Honan Revolutionary Committee, Chou En-lai is well known and usually classed as a moderate, Li Hsien-nien is a deputy premier and Minister of Finance, Li Hsüeh-feng is an old Party man and currently Chairman of the Hopeh Revolutionary Committee, and Tung Pi-wu is one of the Party's old guard, aged eighty-three, and a Vice-Chairman of the PRC. Overall, the new Politburo represents an extremely diverse grouping, with the military as the dominant section and the chief beneficiary of the Cultural Revolution.

Little can be gauged concerning the status of other Central Party organs. The Secretariat was not referred to directly in the Party constitution, and of its former membership of thirteen, nine were purged in the course of the Cultural Revolution, including the General Secretary Teng Hsiao-p'ing, as well as Lo Jui-ch'ing, Lu Ting-yi and P'eng Chen. The only four former Secretariat members who are still in positions of some political prominence are K'ang Sheng, Li Fu-ch'un, Li Hsien-nien, and Li Hsüeh-feng.

Of the known departments of the Central Committee, ten departmental heads were purged, and only one, Ts'ai Ch'ang (head of the Women's Department and wife of Li Fu-ch'un), was reportedly still active in 1969.

The Party Control Commission was also not referred to in

the new constitution, and it was estimated that of the sixty members of the former Central Control Commission, only six survived, among them the head of the Commission, Tung Pi-wu.[11]

It is probable, in the light of the reconstruction of the Party, that all these organs, or their equivalents, will be re-established. Since they will be under the direct control of the Standing Committee of the Politburo, however, rather than the Politburo itself (as in the 1956 Party constitution), they will be subject to stricter central control.

Only a skeleton organisation exists for the Party under the Central levels. Of the six regional bureaux of the Central Committee, only one of the Party secretaries survived the purge (Li Hsüeh-feng). Of the estimated 270 secretaries at regional and provincial levels in 1966, only some 15 per cent made reported appearances during 1967, while 30 per cent suffered serious criticism, and over 50 per cent are no longer referred to in news reports. Truly, it might be said that the revolution has devoured its children.

[11] *China News Analysis,* no. 757 (16 May 1969), p. 6.

3

THE STATE STRUCTURE

On 1 October 1949 Mao Tse-tung formally announced the creation of the People's Republic of China (PRC). Among the tasks facing the Chinese Communist Party was an ambitious programme of rehabilitating China's war-torn economy and the stimulation of economic growth by large-scale investment in heavy industry, plus agrarian reform, combined with widespread social change. In order to accomplish these aims, the Party had to establish a new administrative apparatus, or state structure, to implement and supervise its policies. In building up the new governmental apparatus, the Party leaders were able to draw not only on the structure they had inherited from the Kuomintang, but also upon their own experiences of ruling the Chinese people during the Kiangsi Soviet period (1930–4) and their later control of the "liberated areas" of China, as well as upon the experience of the Soviet Union.

Chinese People's Political Consultative Conference

On paper, the most important government institution during the early years of the PRC was the Chinese People's Political Consultative Conference (CPPCC), which first met from 21–30 September. Present were 584 formal and 77 candidate (non-voting) delegates. The formal delegates represented political parties, geographical areas, people's organisations, religious groups, national minorities and the overseas Chinese. The fact that the largest bloc of delegates was that representing, not the political parties, but the people's organisations (such as the All China Federation of Democratic Women) showed the importance attached to these groups by the Party. The CPPCC passed three documents: a Common Programme, an Organic Law of the CPPCC, and an Organic Law of the Central People's Government. As the delegates were all either Communist Party members or supported their policies, there were no dissenting opinions, and all laws and resolutions were passed unanimously.

Of the three documents adopted by the CPPCC, the Common Programme was the most important, as it embodied the basic aims of the Chinese leaders during the transition of China to socialism. As stated in its Preamble, the political basis of China was to be that of "New Democracy", exercised by a "People's Democratic Dictatorship". "New Democracy" referred to the transitional stage through which China was about to pass between "semi-feudalism" and "semi-colonialism", and the future proletarian dictatorship. Because of the weakness of the working class, socialism could not be implemented at once, so the workers would therefore share power as part of a four-class bloc, composed of the peasants, petty (or less wealthy) bourgeoisie, and national bourgeoisie (owners of enterprises and businessmen uninvolved with Western imperialism), in which the workers, with their allies the peasants, would play the leading role. As the vanguard of the working class, the CCP would, of course, be the directing brain behind "New Democracy". Under this four-class bloc "People's Democratic Dictatorship", as spelt out by Mao Tse-tung in his article of that title written in 1949, meant that democracy would be given to members of the "people", that is, workers, peasants and the petty and national bourgeoisie, but "dictatorship" would be exercised over the others—the bureaucrat capitalists (big bourgeoisie allied with the KMT), feudal landlords and other enemies of the people. When referring to electoral rights and the freedoms of speech and thought the Common Programme clearly laid down that these were for the "people" only.

The Common Programme, after stipulating several basic policy lines, such as the abolition of imperialist privileges, land reform, the need to industrialise, equal rights for all national minorities, and friendship with the USSR—stated that the CPPCC was a provisional organ which would only exercise state power until such time as a National People's Congress was elected by all the voters. During this interim period, which was to last until 1954 the CPPCC would exercise the powers of the National People's Congress, and would elect a Central People's Government Council. The CPPCC then elected a National Committee of 180 to carry out the functions of the CPPCC in between its plenary sessions, and a Standing Committee of twenty to perform the same function when the National Committee was not in session.

The Organic Law of the CPPCC stated that it was the aim of the CPPCC to unite all democratic classes and nationalities throughout China by establishing the unity of all democratic parties and groups, and people's organisations. The CPPCC would carry out the programme of New Democracy, oppose imperialism, feudalism and bureaucrat capitalism, overthrow the Kuomintang, and eliminate counter-revolutionaries. Finally, it would build up the economy, and establish a strong, independent and peaceful People's Republic of China. All democratic parties and groups, and people's organisations which subscribed to these aims were to be permitted to take part in the CPPCC, providing they were approved by its National Committee. Individuals could also be selected by the National Committee. Furthermore, it was the responsibility of the National Committee to select the units and individuals to attend CPPCC plenums, and to determine the size of the delegations. However, on the termination of its September 1949 session, the CPPCC ceased to play a major part, the role of supreme governmental organ passing to the newly elected Central People's Government Council.

Central People's Government Council and Government Administration Council 1949–54

The Central People's Government Council (CPGC) had a total of fifty-six members, including a Chairman and six Vice-Chairmen, and was simultaneously a legislative, executive and judicial organ. The prime initial task of the CPGC was to set up a number of subordinate organs of state, of which the most important was the Government Administration Council (GAC), a kind of super-Cabinet composed of a Premier, five Deputy Premiers, a Secretary General and sixteen members. Although all the economic and other ministries fell under the GAC, the GAC members were not all necessarily ministers. Instead, under the GAC were four committees to which the ministries were responsible. These were

he Committees of Political and Legal Affairs, Finance and
Economics, Culture and Education, and People's Supervision
(see Table 3). No ministries were allocated to the Committee
of People's Supervision, which was concerned with checking
the way in which ministries and government officials carried
out their duties. Like the members of the GAC, all the heads
of committees and all ministers were appointed by the CPGC.

In addition to the GAC, the CPGC also set up a Revolutionary Military Council as the highest military organ of the
state; a Supreme Court as the highest judicial organ; and a
Supreme People's Procuracy which was to supervise the observance of the law by all government offices and personnel.
The CPGC had the right to appoint and dismiss the heads
and leading members of all these bodies.

Both the CPGC and the GAC were more powerful government organs than the CPPCC, which theoretically possessed supreme legislative power. However, they too only
implemented decisions already taken by the Communist Party,
which maintained its control over the government by having
its own personnel in key positions. Mao Tse-tung for example
was Chairman of both the CPPCC's National and Standing
Committees, as well as of the CPGC. He therefore combined
the leadership of both Party and state. Chou En-lai, a member
of the CCP Politburo, was made Premier of the GAC. All
the other members of the government were carefully selected
by the Party.

The governmental apparatus, however, was more than just
a façade or front for the Communist Party. Apart from being
a necessary administrative apparatus for the execution of
Party policies, such organisations as the CPPCC and lower-
level governmental bodies drew large segments of the people
into some minimal form of political participation, and allowed the Party to sound out the opinions and attitudes of
the intellectuals, businessmen and other key sectors of the
population.

Before adjourning on 30 September the CPPCC plenum
passed resolutions on a national anthem and national flag
(red background with five gold stars, one large star for the
CCP and four small stars representing the four classes making up the "people"), and changed the name of Peip'ing (or

CENTRAL GOVERNMENT ORGANIZATION 1949-1954

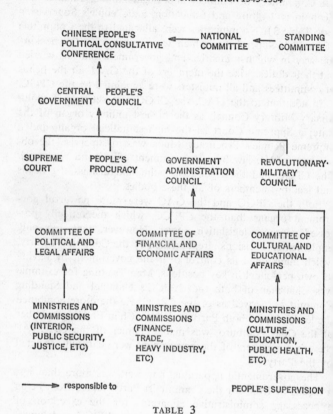

TABLE 3

"northern plain") back to Peking ("northern capital"). On
1 October 1949 Mao Tse-tung formally proclaimed the establishment of the People's Republic of China.

Administrative areas

China's vast size, great population, and diverse peoples and
geographical conditions, coupled with relatively poor communication facilities, made it necessary in 1949 for the government to create six Great Administrative Areas interposed

between the central government and the provinces. Each Great Administrative Area controlled a number of provinces. A separate Autonomous Region was established for Inner Mongolia, and the status of Tibet was left undetermined. The six Great Administrative Areas were as follows:

(1) North China: Chahar, Hopeh, P'ingyuan (a new area formed from fifty-six counties detached from the provinces of Honan, Hopeh and Shantung), Shansi, Suiyuan. (The North China Great Administrative Area was directly administered by the central government.)

(2) North-east: Liaotung, Liaohsi, Kirin, Sunkiang, Heilunkiang, Jehol. (The six provinces making up Manchuria.)

(3) North-west: Chinghai, Kansu, Ninghsia, Shensi, Sinkiang.

(4) South-west: Kweichow, Sikang, North, South, East and West Szechuan, Yunnan.

(5) East China: North and South Anhwei, Chekiang, Fukien, North and South Kiangsu, Shantung.

(6) Central-South: Honan, Hupeh, Hunan, Kiangsi, Kwangtung, Kwangsi.

These six areas differed greatly in their degree of industrial and economic development, and in their previous exposure to communist rule. The North-eastern area (Manchuria) was the most advanced economically (although much of its industrial equipment had been removed by the Russians after their brief occupation of the area at the end of the Second World War), and much of it had been "liberated" by the communists well before 1949. A similar situation, although to a lesser degree, prevailed in the Northern and Eastern regions. The other parts of the country were very backward, however, particularly in the North-western and Southwestern areas.

As initially set up at the end of 1949, the six Great Administrative Areas had military governments, usually led by a seasoned communist military commander. Their organisation was modelled on that of the Central People's Government Council, and they all had a Government Council which ran three committees, under which the various ministries were grouped. Most of the leading personnel of the Great Administrative Areas' governments were proposed by the Government Administration Council in Peking, and appointed by the CPGC.

Because of this administrative decentralisation from Peking, and because of the variform natures of their regions, the Administrative Areas tended to develop a degree of local autonomy, initiating some local policies, and interpreting central directives to suit their own conditions. But their degree of local independence should not be overestimated, as Peking often sent them detailed instructions.

Nevertheless, the degree of local autonomy involved proved to be too great for the leaders in Peking, and from 1952 onwards, the powers of the Great Administrative Areas were gradually curtailed, leading to their abolition in 1954. The first step in this process came on 19 November 1952 when the CPGC ordered that civilians should take over from the military governments. This was done by early 1953. The same order also reduced the status of the ministries in the Great Administrative Areas to that of "local government offices", and transferred some of the ministries to the jurisdiction of Peking. The eventual doom of the Great Administrative Areas was foreshadowed in the Election Law published in February 1953, which laid down the procedures to be followed at the various administrative levels for sending delegates up to the National People's Congress. No reference was made in the Law to the Great Administrative Areas.

This evoked opposition from some of the Chairmen of the Great Administrative Areas. In February 1954 criticism was made of them at a meeting of the Central Committee of the Communist Party, the resolution of which spoke of men who ruled their areas like "independent kingdoms". Kao Kang, Chairman of the North-eastern area, promptly disappeared from sight, followed by the purge of Jao Shu-shih, boss of the Eastern area, a short while later. Both Kao and Jao had apparently tried to use their regional power bases to implement Soviet-style economic policies and to increase their power in Peking.

The Great Administrative Areas were formally abolished on 19 June 1954 at a meeting of the Central People's Gov-

ernment Council. The official reason given was that they were
impeding the efforts of the central government to monitor
the situation in the provinces and cities. In fact, they represented too great an independent power to the Party leaders
in Peking. With their abolition, the provincial governments
came under the direct control of the centre. However, the
Great Administrative Areas were resurrected in a very
limited form in 1961, with the formation of regional bureaux
of the Central Committee of the CCP, which carried out some
governmental functions.

Lower-level units under the Great Administrative Areas
during the 1949–54 period comprised provinces, special
districts, counties, districts and administrative villages (see
Table 4). The province and the county were the two most important levels. Immediately after the founding of the People's
Republic, several of the existing provinces were split up into
two or more units. Anhwei was divided into North Anhwei
and South Anhwei, as was Kiangsu. Szechuan was divided
into four: North, South, East and West; and a new provincial
unit, P'ingyuan, was created from counties separated from
other provinces. Three new provinces were produced in Manchuria, making six in all. This trend was reversed at the same
time as the curtailment of the powers of the Great Administrative Areas. In November 1952 P'ingyuan was removed
from the map, with the majority of its component parts reverting to their original provinces. Chahar was also scrapped,
with its counties joined on to contiguous provinces. During
1952–3 the provinces of Anhwei, Kiangsu and Szechuan,
previously divided, were re-formed into single units. This
movement towards fewer but larger provincial units continued
in 1954 with the abolition of Suiyuan in March, the incor-
poration of Ninghsia into Kansu in June, and the reduction
of Manchuria to its original three provinces (Liaoning, Kirin
and Heilungkiang) in August, thus reducing the number of
provinces from thirty-five to twenty-four. Further reductions
were to follow in 1955.

Under the provinces came the special districts, numbering
from five to fourteen to a province, under each of which
several counties were grouped. Although they were not mentioned in the 1954 Constitution, the special districts neverthe-

less continued to exist. Immediately under the special districts came the counties, many of which were considerably altered in size to suit the administrative convenience of the communists after 1949. The number of counties in China was drastically reduced by the administrative changes of the communisation movement of 1958–9, but reverted to their previous number at the end of the Great Leap Forward.

Each county was composed of a number of districts, each of which in turn was made up of a group of administrative villages (*hsiang*). An administrative village, or *hsiang,* was a collection of actual villages. The *hsiang* remained the lowest administrative unit until it was replaced by the commune in 1958. The gradual disappearance of the district after 1955, as an intermediate unit between the *hsiang* and the county, was hastened in 1958 with the inauguration of the Great Leap Forward and the setting up of the communes, each of which absorbed several *hsiang.* However, the collapse of the Great Leap the following year and the reduction in size of the communes was correlated with the gradual re-emergence of the district.

In areas inhabited by national minority groups (i.e. non-Han Chinese), autonomous administrative units were set up. The highest of these was the Autonomous Region, of which there was only one, Inner Mongolia, in 1949. Four other areas, including Sinkiang and Tibet, later qualified for this status. There were a few Autonomous Areas in existence in 1950, which were equivalent in status to the special district, and came under the authority of the provincial government. These were followed in 1952 by other autonomous areas on the county level, responsible to the special district. In 1954, the new Constitution introduced autonomous *chou* (equivalent to the special district), autonomous counties, and even nationality *hsiang* in some counties, to cater for small national minority groups living in a predominantly Chinese area. In spite of the name, little autonomy is granted to the national minority governments. Unlike the USSR, China does not have a federal system of government, and the nationalities have no separate representation at the central government level. On the local level, they are permitted to use the language of the region, and to keep up local customs and dress. Since 1949, however, the tendency has been for the national minorities to be absorbed into the Chinese mainstream, often by the emigration of Han Chinese to the national minority areas, or by including administrative areas inhabited by Han Chinese into autonomous units, thus diluting the concentration of national minority groups. Thus, when Suiyuan was incorporated into Inner Mongolia, there were then more Chinese than Mongols in the area.

Some of the larger cities of China fell outside the normal administrative chain of command. In 1949 fourteen of these cities were under the direct jurisdiction of the Great Administrative Area, rather than the provincial government. In 1954, however, with the abolition of the Great Administrative Areas, all but three, Peking, Shanghai and Tientsin (designated special cities and linked directly to the central government), were placed under the control of the local provincial government. Tientsin was also placed under provincial control in 1958. In addition to these special cities, there were also towns coming under the direct jurisdiction of the special district.

Progress towards a constitution

According to the Common Programme of 1949, the CPPCC was only an interim institution that would exercise power until such time as a National People's Congress, elected by universal franchise, would take over. When established, the National People's Congress (NPC) would ratify a new state constitution of the People's Republic of China.

The holding of a general election to convene the NPC required that, first of all, local units of government be created to carry out elections at the village and city levels, and then on up through the province to the national level. During their conquest of the mainland, however, the communists initially set up, not elected local governments, but military occupations. In the towns, Military Control Commissions were formed, responsible for controlling the newspapers and radio stations, the police, banks, transport and communications, education and industrial production. In the case of Peking, for example, military rule was imposed in January 1949, after the conclusion of a peace treaty between the

ADMINISTRATIVE DIVISIONS 1949-1954

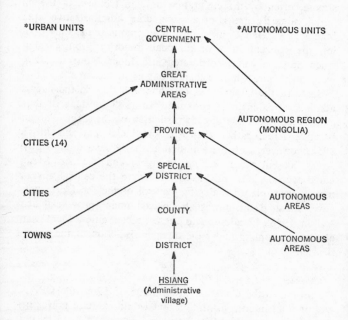

*EACH URBAN AND AUTONOMOUS UNIT HAD
ITS OWN ADMINISTRATIVE SUB-DIVISIONS

⟶ responsible to

TABLE 4

Kuomintang general Fu Tso-yi, and Lin Piao for the communists. The chief of the Military Control Commission for Peking, Yeh Chien-ying, then handed over power in February to a fledgling Peking municipal government, under the chairmanship of—Yeh Chien-ying.

In the rural areas, at the village, district and county levels, the local Red Army command set up "people's governments", largely staffed by army men. The Communist Party itself organised the government at the provincial and city levels. By commencing their administration in a planned, orderly and disciplined manner, by restoring order and halting inflation, the communists went a long way towards securing at least the tacit support of many Chinese, exhausted by the chaos and corruption of twelve years of almost constant war.

At the end of 1949, these interim arrangements in both urban and rural areas were replaced at county, municipal and provincial levels by People's Conferences, which were consultative bodies modelled on the CPPCC, whose members were nominated by the local authorities, together with additional members elected by people's organisations under the control of the communists. Their functions were limited, and can be summarised as the transmission of orders, reporting of results and the guiding of work. Since they had only limited power, people were generally apathetic in their approach to them, and it was only by 1951 that most of the counties had held People's Conferences. However, by 1950 the system had been extended to the district and village, and by 1952 the majority of People's Conferences at all levels had elected a local government.

According to article 14 of the Common Programme, the People's Conferences were only in power pending the creation of local People's *Congresses,* to be elected by universal franchise. Elections were to be held as soon as possible, once military operations had been completed, agrarian reform thoroughly carried out, and People's Conferences set up.

On 24 December 1952 Chou En-lai, representing the Central Committee of the CCP, proposed on behalf of the Communist Party that the country should prepare to conduct elections in 1953, preparatory to convening the first NPC in October of that year. He said that this had not been undertaken in 1949 because at that time the "people's liberation war had not been concluded, the basic political and social reforms had not been carried out on a national scale, and the economy still called for a period of consolidation". By the end of 1952, however, China was completely "liberated" (with the exception of Taiwan), agrarian reform had been successfully carried out (although not in the national minority areas), and a number of political ideological campaigns launched by the Party had "consolidated the economic, political and ideological leadership of the working-class". Finally, the temporary system of People's Conferences had been extended over the whole country.

Accordingly, the CPGC adopted a resolution on 13 January 1953, which concurred in the above reasoning, and said that elections were to take place at the administrative village, county, provincial and municipal levels so as to convene People's Congresses, following which a National People's Congress would be held, to enact a constitution, ratify the Five-year economic plan, and elect a new central government. At the same time, a committee was nominated under the chairmanship of Chou En-lai to prepare an Election Law. This was ready by 11 February and promulgated by the CPGC on 1 March 1953.

All people over the age of eighteen had the right to vote and be elected as a deputy, regardless of nationality, race, sex, occupation, social origin, religion, education, property status or residence. Excluded were unreformed landlords, counter-revolutionaries, lunatics, and "others who have been deprived of their electoral rights according to law", which also included all those who fell outside the ranks of the four classes comprising the "people". The election was on a hierarchical basis, with the population playing a direct role only at the lowest levels. At these basic levels, namely the *hsiang*, small town, and municipal district, the voters directly elected their candidates to the local People's Congress. From then on, however, delegates to higher People's Congresses at the county, city and provincial levels were indirectly elected by the lower-level People's Congresses. The number of delegates to a small town or *hsiang* People's Congress was expected to range from fifteen to thirty-five (the actual count being determined by the population of the unit), and 100–500 in the case of a provincial People's Congress, resulting in a total of approximately 1,200 deputies present at the National People's Congress. This last figure included deputies from the national minorities, the armed forces and the overseas Chinese.

The Electoral Law specified that a Central Election Committee should be appointed by the CPGC, and that local Election Committees should be appointed by the governments at the next higher level. In practice, the county governments trained electoral workers, who went into the villages and chose suitable people for the Election Committee. The CPGC appointed twenty-nine people to the Central Election Committee on 11 February under the chairmanship of Liu Shao-ch'i. The functions of this body were to supervise the progress of the election by directing the work of the local Election Committees. The functions of these local committees were to conduct the registration of those qualified to vote, publish the candidates' list, demarcate the electoral districts, fix the date of the election, convene and conduct the election meeting, and finally, to count the ballots and determine who had been elected.

The voting at all levels except the lowest was to be by secret ballot. At the basic levels, where the population was directly involved, it was laid down that voting could be conducted either by a secret ballot, or by a show of hands, and that as a rule a show of hands would be used. This facilitated close Party supervision. Candidates were to be nominated by the Communist Party, the democratic parties, people's organisations, or individuals. The list of candidates was determined at a joint meeting of these organisations, and invariably the number of candidates proposed was identical with the number of deputies needed.

The NPC, slated to convene in Peking in October 1953, was not destined to meet until September 1954. The local elections were postponed in September 1953, when April 1954 was fixed as the latest date for the holding of county People's Congresses, and then again delayed in April 1954 for two months when June was set as the latest date for the counties, and July-August for the city and provincial levels. The delays in the elections were probably due to the slow progress made in the villages. Nevertheless, by July 1954, all the deputies to provincial and city Congresses had been elected (a total of 16,806), and the First National People's Congress convened in Peking from 15 to 28 September with 1,141 deputies present.

The most vital tasks of the NPC were the adoption of a Constitution to replace the temporary Common Programme, and the election of the officials of the new government. A committee for drafting the Constitution had been set up in January 1953, under the chairmanship of Mao Tse-tung. In March 1954 this committee accepted a draft submitted to it by the Central Committee of the CCP, which for the next two months was discussed by some 8,000 people representing the democratic parties and people's organisations. The text of this draft Constitution was published on 14 June 1954, and it was claimed that more than 150 million people took part in discussions of it, with many suggested amendments or revisions. On the basis of these suggestions, a very slightly revised draft was adopted by the CPGC on 9 September 1954, and submitted to the NPC where it was approved unanimously and without alteration on 20 September.

The Constitution

The Preamble declared that China was now in a transitional stage of progressing towards a socialist society, and that the Constitution reflected the requirements of the state during this period of transition. Accordingly, the heading of General Principles which began the Constitution dealt mainly with the differing types of ownership of the means of production, which were divided into four: state ownership, cooperative ownership, ownership by individual working people and capitalist ownership. Article 10, while giving legal protection to the right of capitalists to own means of production, also went on to add that "the policy of the state towards capitalist industry and commerce is to use, restrict and transform them". Feudal landlords and bureaucrat capitalists were deprived of political rights, but permitted to seek reform through labour (article 19). Policy towards the rich peasant economy was "to restrict and gradually eliminate it".

Under the heading of Fundamental Rights and Duties of Citizens came nineteen articles granting equality before the law, freedom of the press, assembly and religious belief, as well as the right to work, leisure, education and sexual equality, balanced by a smaller number of duties which included obedience to the law, paying of taxes and military service. The Communist Party was given no legal standing by the Constitution. Indeed the Party was mentioned but twice in the whole document, both times in the Preamble, and only with reference to its leadership of the Chinese people before 1949.

Central government organisation

The body of the Constitution covered the organisational structure of the government, something which is normally absent from Western constitutions. Although in a sense the Constitution of the PRC is only a façade whereby the Party legitimises its own right to rule, nevertheless an understanding of the Constitution, and so of the state structure, is essential as an insight into the organisations through which the Party executes its commands.

Article 3 stated that China was a unitary, multi-national state, or in other words, that China had a single chamber legislature, instead of a separate Chamber of Nationalities as in the Soviet Union. The government was discussed by the Constitution under three headings—the legislature or National People's Congress, the Chairman of the People's Republic or its head of state, and the State Council or Cabinet. The NPC was said to be the sole legislative organ, which was actually the case only in a theoretical sense, since the term "laws" did not include the decrees of the Standing Committee of the NPC, the decisions and orders of the State Council, or the decisions of the Communist Party, all of which had the force of law.

With the ratification of the Constitution, the CPPCC became a purely advisory organ, although it has maintained a vestigial existence to this day. Constitutionally, the NPC became the highest organ of state power. It is elected for a period of four years, normally meets once a year for only a few days at a time, and is too big a body to arrive at major decisions itself. Constitutionally it has the right to elect the Chairman and Vice-Chairman of the PRC, choose the Premier of the State Council (on the recommendation of the Chairman of the PRC), the members of the State Council (on the recommendation of the Premier), and other government officials. The NPC has the power to remove from office the Chairman and Vice-Chairman of the PRC, the Premier and members of the State Council and others. In addition, the NPC approves or decides on the national economic plan, the state budget and questions of war and peace. In fact, it is primarily a "rubber-stamp" body which exercises no initiatives in policy.

During its first session, the NPC elected a Standing Committee. This body, which normally meets twice a month, is extremely important on paper. It conducts elections for the NPC and convenes NPC sessions, interprets laws and makes decrees, supervises the work of the State Council, and annuls orders and decisions of the State Council which contravene the Constitution, as well as having the power to annul "inappropriate" decisions of lower-governmental organs. In addition, it decides on the appointment and removal of Vice-Premiers and Ministers of the State Council when the NPC is not in session, as well as various members of the Supreme Court and the Procuracy. Liu Shao-ch'i was elected the Chairman of the NPC Standing Committee in 1954, and it had a total membership of sixty-five. Politically its membership was not impressive, since many of its members (thirty-one, including the Dalai Lama) did not belong to the Communist Party. In effect, the NPC and its Standing Committee only gave constitutional legitimacy to decisions and policies already determined by the top Party leadership. In addition, by means of elections and the sending of deputies from all over the nation to Peking, the NPC sessions gave the mass of the people a sense of involvement with the regime (over five million were elected to the People's Congresses at the lowest levels), gave local political activists the possibility of increased prestige by becoming an NPC deputy, and acted as a symbol of national solidarity.

Mao Tse-tung maintained his position as chief of state in 1954 by being elected Chairman of the PRC by the Congress. (In 1959 Mao was replaced by Liu Shao-ch'i. According to a CCP Central Committee resolution of November 1968, Liu was removed from all his Party and government posts. Formally, however, he would retain his position as head of state until the resolution was ratified by a meeting of the NPC.) On paper, the Chairman's functions were not particularly impressive. Mainly procedural in nature, they consisted primarily of acting on decisions already reached by other bodies. Constitutionally, however, he was commander of the armed forces and Chairman of the Council of National Defence. In addition, he could "whenever necessary" convene a Supreme State Conference, composed of the PRC Vice-Chairman (Chu Teh at that time, but Tung Pi-wu and Soong Ch'ing-ling since 1959), the Chairman of the NPC Standing Committee (Liu Shao-ch'i, and then Chu Teh after 1959), the Premier of the State Council (Chou En-lai) and others.

The former Government Administration Council was replaced by the State Council, or Cabinet, under the control of its Premier, Chou En-lai. In addition to the Premier, the full Cabinet included ten Vice-Premiers, a Secretary General and the heads of thirty Ministries and five Commissions. As this was too large a body to function well, provision was made for an "inner Cabinet" composed of the Premier, Vice-Premiers and Secretary General, which would conduct the day-to-day work of government. Of these twelve men, only one was not a full member of the Party's Central Committee. (This was Ulanfu, who was an alternate member of the Central Committee and Secretary of the Inner Mongolian Bureau of the CCP.) This is a good example of what has been called "the law of the vanishing united front", which states that in any non-Party organisation, the more powerful it is, the fewer will be the number of non-communists.[1] In the case of the Standing Committee of the NPC, just over 50 per cent of its membership were Party members; this was increased to over two-thirds in the case of the State Council and rose to 100 per cent in the case of the "inner Cabinet".

The State Council is the leading executive agency of the government, responsible primarily for economic management through its command of the various ministries and commissions under it. It meets, on average, about once a month. Among other duties, the Constitution gave it the functions of coordinating and leading the work of the ministries, carrying out the economic plan and the state budget, and administering foreign and domestic trade. Organisational changes from the former Government Administration Council were not great: three new ministries were added, and some new commissions

[1] See, for example, Dennis J. Doolin and Robert C. North, *The Chinese People's Republic* (Stanford, California: The Hoover Institution on War, Revolution and Peace, 1966), p. 64, fn. 6.

created. The most important change was the abolition of the three Cabinet Committees which formerly came between the Cabinet and the ministries. However, with the setting up in November 1954 of eight Cabinet Bureaux (not shown on Table 5), the previous system was virtually restored, as the Bureaux, like their predecessors, were primarily bodies through which the Communist Party supervised the activities of groups of ministries carrying out related kinds of work.

Parallel to the State Council, and responsible to the NPC were set up the Supreme People's Court, the highest judicial organ, under its President Tung Pi-wu, and the Supreme People's Procuracy, whose task was to ensure that the activities of government organs conformed to the law. The new Chief Procurator was Chang Ting-ch'eng. The former Revolutionary Military Council was abolished and replaced by a Ministry of Defence under the State Council. Also provided for was a new long-range planning body, the Council of National Defence under the chairmanship of Mao Tse-tung, and separate from the State Council.

CENTRAL GOVERNMENT ORGANIZATION 1954-

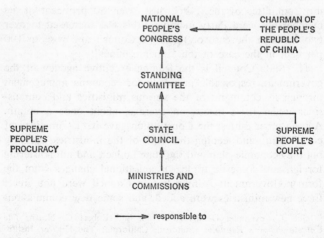

TABLE 5

Elections for delegates to a new National People's Congress were held in 1958, and the second NPC met in April 1959. The major event of this session was the relinquishing by Mao Tse-tung of his post of Chairman of the Republic to Liu Shao-ch'i, who was his heir-apparent at that time. Ostensibly, this move was made to give Mao more time to devote to political and ideological work, but it was later claimed (1966) that he was forced into giving up the post by an anti-Mao group under the leadership of Liu. Mao was in fact obliged to fade temporarily into the background, because of the failure of his policy of the Great Leap Forward. Liu was completely discredited during the course of the Great Proletarian Cultural Revolution. He was removed from all his Party and state posts in 1968, but at the present time of writing he is still formally China's head of state. Other changes made at the second NPC included the transfer of Chu Teh from Vice-Chairman of the Republic to the Chairmanship of the NPC Standing Committee (replacing Liu Shao-ch'i), and the increase in the number of Vice-Chairmanships of the Republic from one to two—Tung Pi-wu and Soong Ch'ing-ling, the widow of Sun Yat-sen.

At the third and most recent session of the NPC in December 1964–January 1965 the number of deputies was more than doubled, to over 3,000. No major personnel changes took place. Since 1954, there have been a number of re-organisations in the economic structure under the State Council, with the number of central ministries roughly doubling over the years. Nevertheless, considerable uniformity of function has been maintained.

Organs of local government

According to the Constitution, the organs of local government parallel the administrative divisions under the central government. Thus the province, county, district, *hsiang,* city district and town each elects its People's Congress. (The special district has no Congress.) Only at the lowest levels are these Congresses directly elected by the population, at the levels of cities not divided into districts, city districts (of cities large enough to be so subdivided), and *hsiang*. At all levels above these, the People's Congresses are elected by the Congresses on the next lower level. Thus the county Congress sends delegates to the provincial Congress. Provincial Congresses are elected for four years, and all the rest for two. The main task of these Congresses, apart from selecting delegates to higher level Congresses, is to elect a local People's Council and other local officials such as the head of the People's Court. In effect, with respect to the election of the People's Council, the Congress just approves a slate of names pre-selected by the local Party committee. Although the Congresses have constitutionally a large number of functions, these are normally undertaken by the People's Council as the executive agency of the Congress, as the Congresses meet infrequently, and then only briefly. At the county and provincial levels, the Councils meet once a month, and at the lower levels, once every two weeks.

Theoretically, every Council is responsible to the Congress on its own level and to the Council on the next higher level. In practice, however, the line of responsibility from the local People's Congress can be ignored, with the actual line of authority extending down the governmental hierarchy from the State Council to the local Councils at the very lowest levels, the *hsiang* in the rural areas and the city or city district elsewhere.

Local government in the countryside

The State Council has the power to alter or annul "inappropriate" decisions issued by any People's Council. In addition, it directly appoints the heads and deputy heads of all the departments under the People's Council at the provincial (and special city) levels. One must also remember at this stage the presence of the ubiquitous Party apparatus which parallels that of the government at every level. Thus a government department on one level will be responsible not only to the corresponding department on the next higher level, but to the Party committee on the same level. For example, the county government Propaganda Department (a unit of the county People's Council), is responsible to both the special district Propaganda Department (of the special district office), *and* to the county Party committee (specifically, to its Propaganda Department). Each local government is therefore subject to two sets of possibly conflicting pressures: one vertically through the government apparatus, up to the corresponding ministry of the State Council, and the other horizontally, through the local Party committee, reaching up to a department of the CCP Central Committee in Peking.

In the local government hierarchy, it is the county level which is particularly important, for this is the lowest level to have the specialised institutions (such as the Propaganda Department in the above example) corresponding to the central ministries in Peking. The People's Council is the top government organisation in the county, paralleled by the county Party committee, with the latter having authority over the former, deciding policy (in the light of directives received from higher Party organs) to be implemented by the government's administrative apparatus. The chief officials of the People's Council, who are themselves usually Party members, meet once a week on average to discuss the routine execution of policy, and they work closely with the Party committee. Some fields of government operations, such as public security or united front work, are run almost entirely by the Party itself. In the case of the government's personnel department, all the staff will most probably belong either to the CCP or the Young Communist League. In reality they will be acting on behalf of the county Party Organisation Department, which means that the Party has a tremendous influence over the county government because of its control over assignments and careers of all Party and non-Party cadres in the government bureaucracy.

With respect to the layers of local government below the county level, these were the districts and *hsiang* (administrative villages) up until the time of the Great Leap Forward. However, during the period before the Great Leap (1949–57), initial steps towards the collectivisation of land were taken by the CCP, commencing in 1950 with Mutual Aid Teams, to each of which between four and nine households belonged. The Mutual Aid Teams were absorbed by lower Agricultural Producers' Cooperatives (APCs) from 1953 onwards, in which the peasants still retained the ownership of their land. By 1955–6, however, the lower APCs were transformed into higher APCs, in which the land was owned collectively. The growth and functions of these production-based organisations led to conflict between them and the territorially organised district and *hsiang* governments, resolved only in 1958 with the creation of the people's communes, which were organised on the basis of the higher APCs and merged with the units of local government (ostensibly with the *hsiang*, but often in fact with the district). The local Party

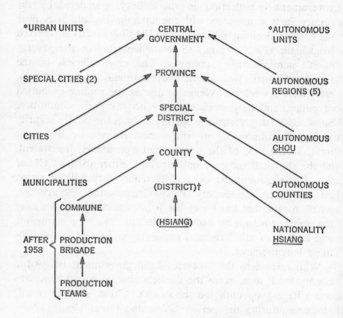

ADMINISTRATIVE DIVISIONS 1954-

*EACH URBAN AND AUTONOMOUS UNIT HAS
ITS OWN ADMINISTRATIVE SUB-DIVISIONS

†WITH THE SHRINKAGE IN SIZE OF THE COMMUNES
AFTER 1960, DISTRICTS RE-EMERGED IN MANY AREAS

———➤ responsible to

TABLE 6

organs also merged with the commune apparatus. Since 1961, however, there has been a tendency for the districts to re-emerge as the role of the communes declined, with the communes, reduced in status, below the district government on the level of the former *hsiang* (see Table 6). At the same time, the former demarcation between government and Party organs, abolished by the creation of the communes, has reappeared.

Urban government

Local government in the cities of China was organised in a different fashion to that in the countryside. In order to facilitate control over the urban population, "urban residents' committees" were gradually introduced into the cities from 1951 onwards, and formally ordered to be set up in all cities by a resolution of the Standing Committee of the NPC adopted in 1954. The urban residents' committees were mass organisations set up under the guidance of the local People's Council. Their tasks were to mobilise the urban population to participate in the government's political campaigns, supervise the activities of subversive elements, carry out public welfare work, and settle neighbourhood quarrels. So as to be more effective in population control, each committee was normally to cover an area coterminous with the local public security (police) office, encompassing 100–600 households. Under each committee, inhabitants' teams of 15–40 households were formed, all with officers elected by the local population under the guidance of the CCP.

Clearly the aim of Peking was to draw into political organisation the large numbers of people in the suburbs, such as housewives and small businessmen, not subject to control and indoctrination through their factory committee or trade union. In addition the regime faced the problem of a tremendous growth in urban population, which had increased by over 40 per cent between 1950 and 1953. This population growth had resulted in a big burden of civil administrative work on the police, much of which was now taken over by the inhabitants' committees and "street offices", the creation of which was also announced at the same time in 1954. These urban street offices, which guided the work of the inhabitants' committees, were set up in all cities having over 50,000 population, and, like the inhabitants' committees, covered the same administrative area as the local police station. Unlike the inhabitants' committees, however, their officers were not elected, but appointed by the People's Council. Both organisations cooperated to relieve the load on the police, and increase the contact between government and population.

In the latter half of 1958, urban people's communes were formed in the cities in imitation of the communes springing up all over the length and breadth of rural China. Partially they were organised on the wave of enthusiasm that greeted the rural communes and the Great Leap Forward that was to usher in "true" communism in China, and partially to help solve the continuing problem of the increasing population growth in the cities. This growth stemmed largely from migration to the cities from the countryside, and had resulted in the urban population increasing from fifty-seven million in 1949 to ninety-two million in 1957, a percentage increase far larger than that for China as a whole. The urban communes were therefore designed to put the city dwellers to work, and thus harness them for economic growth. Like their rural counterparts, the urban communes were to be integrated economic, social and military organs. However, they were short-lived, for they were soon caught by the wave of caution that followed doubts concerning the over-optimistic predictions of the Great Leap. Although continuing in name, and as economic units, after 1959 they ceased to function as their original concept of an integrated unit.

Recent changes

With the advent of the Cultural Revolution, there has been considerable disorder and reorganisation at all levels of the state structure. Many top Party leaders (and therefore top government officials) fell in the repeated purges, and meetings of such bodies as the plenums of the State Council[2] and the NPC Standing Committee have not been held since early 1966. Government organisations at all levels were swept away by the Red Guards and general chaos of 1966, and it was

[2] It has been announced that the State Council met in March 1970.

only in the following year that some attempt was made to reconstruct them in a new form.

The administrative divisions have remained largely unchanged, except for the increased importance of the Military Regions interposed between the provincial level and Peking. Each of these is named after a city, and all but one comprises several provinces. In addition, there are three areas, Sinkiang, Tibet and Inner Mongolia, which are not attached to any Military Regions. The Military Regions are on the same administrative level as the Party's Regional Bureaux, but do not cover the same geographical areas. Their prominence reflects the growth in power of Lin Piao and the increased intrusion of the military into administrative affairs at all levels of the country.

With the reconstruction of the administrative apparatus, each unit (school, factory or commune) and every level (administrative village, district, county, special district and province) was ordered to set up a revolutionary committee. Each revolutionary committee was to be formed with the help of the People's Liberation Army, and composed of a three-way alliance of the Army, the pro-Mao young radicals (mainly Red Guards or Revolutionary Rebels), and the remnants of the local Party and government officials. At the key level of the province, the first Revolutionary Committee was created in January 1967, and the rest had all followed suit (after many clashes and setbacks) by September 1968. The role of the military is dominant in all the provincial Revolutionary Committees. The People's Liberation Army also has great influence over the management of the factories, and is active in the countryside. However, with the declining virulence of the Cultural Revolution, "old cadres" (former officials) have been re-emerging at all levels of Party and government.

4

THE ORGANS OF CONTROL AND DEFENCE

Every communist party-state must maintain the necessary organs to ensure the continuance of party rule, and to protect the state against any potential opposition, real or imaginary. Firm political control is particularly essential when the Party wishes to execute large-scale programmes of economic and social reform. The Chinese political system possesses many overlapping control organs which check on the discipline of Party members, supervise the administration of the state, and observe the legality of its citizens' behaviour.

The Party itself is the chief checking organ of the political system, with the discipline of Party members supervised by the Party's network of Control Commissions. Civilian agencies of control include the procuracy, courts and public security apparatus. (The Ministry of Supervision was abolished in 1959.) There are also the formal military organs of control, the People's Liberation Army (PLA) and the militia.

Party Control Commissions

Party Control Commissions were first set up in 1955, replacing the former Commissions for Disciplinary Investigation which had been operating since 1949. The Control Commissions concern themselves only with discipline within the Party: according to the 1956 Party constitution, their tasks were as follows —"regularly to examine and deal with cases of violation of the Party constitution, Party discipline, Communist ethics, and the state laws and decrees on the part of Party members; to decide on or cancel disciplinary measures against Party members; and to deal with appeals and complaints from Party members" (article 53).

The Central Control Commission was set up by a plenary meeting of the Central Committee, with local commissions formed by and working under the direction of local Party

committees. Control Commissions at all levels were strength-
ened in 1962, and the membership of the Central Control
Commission was enlarged. However, the Central Control
Commission was decimated by the Cultural Revolution, although its head, Tung Pi-wu, survived. The new Party constitution passed at the Ninth Congress made no reference to
Control Commissions.

Ministry of Supervision (1949–59)

The Ministry of Supervision (known from 1949 to 1954 as
the Committee of People's Supervision) was an organ designed to check on the correct execution of Party policies
within government agencies. The Ministry had branches in all
government organs and supervised cadres' activities. The
Ministry investigated malpractices, and recommended punishment or further enquiries to be undertaken by other agencies
such as the procuracy. The lines of responsibility between the
Ministry of Supervision, the procuracy and the public security
apparatus became blurred, and it was probably for this reason
that the Ministry was abolished in the general rationalisation
of control organs that took place in 1959.

Political and legal departments

In the late 1950s, the Party was facing the problem of having
to separate the tangled lines of responsibility resulting from
the overlapping functions of the courts, procuracy, and public
security forces. In addition, the Party had found that the
legal system was not immune from trends towards professionalism and dislike of Party domination. With the 100 Flowers
campaign of 1957, many legal figures criticised Party interference in legal work, and demanded more independence.
Those who spoke out were, like other intellectuals, denounced
as "rightists" in the latter half of the year, and the pendulum
swung once more towards "politics in command".

The setting up of Party Political and Legal Departments in
1959 was an attempt to solve both problems.[1]

1 Available refugee information relates only the establishment of these
departments in certain areas, and it can only be assumed that they became nation-wide. See A. Doak Barnett, *Cadres, Bureaucracy and Political Power in Communist China*, pp. 194–7, 219–20. Also Jerome Cohen,

At the county level, the Political and Legal Department was a Party leadership fraction composed of the heads of the county court, procuracy and public security service, presided over by a senior Party member. The Party was therefore in a position to ensure control over the whole legal system of the county, and to coordinate the work of the various government agencies involved. Charges to be brought against alleged criminals, and the sentences to be imposed upon them, were predetermined by the Political and Legal Department in advance of any formal, open, legal proceedings.

The procuracy

The procuracy has a wide range of responsibilities concerning the supervision of legality throughout the country. Article 81 of the State Constitution states that it "ensure(s) observance of the law by all the departments under the State Council, local organs of state at various levels, persons working in organs of state and citizens". The Supreme People's Procuracy was set up in 1954, and is responsible to the National People's Congress, or its Standing Committee, which is charged with supervising the work of the procuracy. The procuracy is also established at local levels of administration down to the county level. It is free from interference by local organs of government since it is responsible, not to the local People's Council, but to the next higher-level procuracy.

The procuracy investigates illegal actions on the part of civil servants and citizens, and issues warrants for arrest where necessary. The procuracy will then initiate formal legal proceedings against criminals and counter-revolutionaries, as well as in civil suits of some prominence. During the court hearings, the procuracy will act as the prosecutor. It also has the general function of supervising court procedure, and may appeal against a decision if it feels it is improper.

From 1959 onwards, with the establishment of Party Political and Legal Departments, the procuracy has become increasingly subordinate to CCP authority, and has lost whatever autonomy it had in earlier years.

"The Party and the Courts: 1949–1959", *China Quarterly*, no. 38 (April–June 1969), pp. 145–7. My information is drawn from these two sources.

The courts

The legal apparatus of Communist China, including the courts, has always been viewed by the Communist Party as an instrument of state policy, for achieving the revolutionary goals of the society and for suppressing those persons considered to be counter-revolutionaries, instead of an instrument used for the protection of individual rights. In his essay *On the People's Democratic Dictatorship*, written in 1949, Mao Tse-tung succinctly stated: "The state apparatus, including the army, the police and the courts, is the instrument by which one class oppresses another. It is an instrument for the oppression of antagonistic classes; it is violence and not 'benevolence'."[2] The administration of justice was particularly violent during the early years of the regime, prior to the enactment of the 1954 state Constitution. During the years 1949–52, when the Party was still consolidating its position, executing the land reform programme and trying to build up a satisfactory judicial system, many cases, especially those which involved the campaign against the landlords in the rural areas, were dealt with by extra-judicial, *ad hoc* "People's Tribunals", which travelled around the country, often meting out the death penalty on landlords and gentry, with sentences carried out immediately. The "People's Tribunals" later moved into the urban areas to help execute the Three- and Five-Anti campaigns, following which they were disbanded. However, they made a temporary reappearance in 1955 with the campaign to suppress counter-revolutionaries, and again more recently during the Cultural Revolution in 1967–8.

With the promulgation of the 1954 Constitution, a formal system of courts was established, with the Supreme People's Court as the highest court, responsible to the National People's Congress, and local courts set up down to county (or municipal district) level, responsible both to the higher level court, and to the local People's Congress. Article 78 of the Constitution proclaimed the independence of the courts, and Chapter Three of the Constitution listed various rights of citi-

---

[2] *Selected Readings from the Works of Mao Tse-tung* (Peking: Foreign Languages Press, 1967), p. 309.

zens which were guaranteed by the state. No provision was made, however, for the Supreme People's Court to declare unconstitutional any act of the government.

The three years following 1954 witnessed a crystallisation of the formal judicial system, and a certain amount of codification of law, although this had only been carried forward to a somewhat limited degree, covering such areas as marriage, agrarian reform and the punishment of counter-revolutionaries, with many disputes continuing to be settled outside the formal judicial apparatus. Nevertheless, the Party largely contented itself with making general policy, in the light of which court cases were to be resolved, rather than having Party officials directly control the courts' decisions. A certain amount of autonomy was therefore granted to the courts, although most cases continued to be handled by extra-judicial administrative arrangements, either by the Party, the public security service or by local "Conciliation Committees". Many routine matters, particularly civil disputes in the realm of property or divorce, were dealt with by these "Conciliation Committees", which attempted to mediate between the parties before a formal legal suit was initiated. These committees therefore lessened the burden on the courts, which handled only criminal and the more important civil cases.

The brief period of liberalisation during the 100 Flowers period of 1957 induced many legal workers to demand greater autonomy for the law, and to criticise Party interference and the slow progress being made towards codification. The Party responded by purging the legal apparatus, and re-emphasising its control over the judiciary. At the same time, the public security apparatus was given increased power to decide cases and impose punishment without the need to seek a court order. In 1959, the Ministry of Justice, which had handled the administration of the courts, was abolished. In the same year, Party Political and Legal Departments were set up, within which the public security apparatus was dominant over the courts and procuracy. These departments normally decided court decisions and sentences in advance, and the courts therefore lost the small amount of autonomy that they had had in earlier years.

Public security

The public security service, or police apparatus, possesses wide-ranging functions and powers that go far beyond the maintenance of law and order. In addition to routine police administration, the public security service is also charged with performing the tasks of census registration, surveillance of overseas Chinese and politically suspect individuals, investigation of criminal cases, border patrol, counter-intelligence work, protection of economic and military installations, monitoring of internal travel, and management of labour reform camps.

From 1957, the public security service, in performing its function of protecting the state against the activities of "counter-revolutionaries" (an ambiguous and broadly-interpreted term), has had the power to arrest suspect individuals and confine them without trial for indefinite periods in labour reform camps.

At the head of the apparatus is the Ministry of Public Security, under the State Council. Local public security bureaux are also set up at lower levels, down to village and urban street administrative units.

The public security bureau plays a special and dominant role within the Party's Political and Legal Departments that were established for the coordination of police and legal work in 1959. The public security bureau is the most powerful of the trio of public security, procuracy and courts that, together with the Party, make up the Political and Legal Department at the county level. This is because it is responsible not to the county People's Council, but to the county Party committee, and because its entire staff is made up of either Party or YCL cadres (which is not the case with any other government bureau with the exception of the Personnel bureau). For this reason, the public security bureau "was regarded by many people as an institution which was basically a Party organ operating within the government bureaucracy . . . or, in other words, even though it was a government bureau, it was viewed as the Party's main instrument for enforcing political control over the population as a whole".[3]

[3] Barnett, op. cit., p. 220.

With the advent of the Cultural Revolution, the work of the public security service was heavily disrupted. The head of the Ministry, Lo Jui-ch'ing, was purged, and replaced by Hsieh Fu-chih. In 1967 the PLA began to increase its influence over the public security apparatus, and during 1967–8 new public security organs, under the control of the PLA, and known as Worker's Provost Corps, made their appearance in certain areas.

People's Liberation Army

At the termination of the civil war with the KMT, the People's Liberation Army numbered some five million men. Although a victorious army, the PLA suffered from severe deficiencies in modern equipment and logistics, deficiencies which were quickly revealed during the early stages of the Korean War, which broke out in 1950 when the North Koreans attacked their southern neighbours. The modernisation of the PLA can be dated from late 1951 when the USSR began supplying substantial quantities of equipment, including tanks, artillery, light arms and jet aircraft. Improvement in the equipment of the PLA continued after the end of the Korean War (in 1953) until 1960, when Soviet aid to China was withdrawn.

There is no completely reliable information on the current strength of the PLA (recruited by means of a conscription system and volunteers), which is estimated by different observers to be in the region of 2–2¾ million men, including naval and air force personnel. The army has over 100 divisions, each of about 15,000 men. The vast majority of these are infantry, with a small number of airborne, anti-aircraft, and artillery divisions. The PLA also has a Railway Corps which has constructed many strategic rail links within China. It is also efficient at repairing supply lines destroyed by bombing, and was so employed during the Korean War, and more recently in Vietnam, where several tens of thousands of construction workers were repairing the rail links between North Vietnam and China.

Following the cessation of Soviet aid, the army has become self-sufficient in light and medium weaponry, but still suffers from shortages of heavy weapons such as armoured equipment.

Air force

The air force experienced rapid growth from the time of the Korean War up until 1960. At that time, their total air strength was estimated at 2,500–3,000 planes, most of these jet fighters of the MIG-15, 17 or 19 range, either supplied by the Soviet Union, or assembled in China with Soviet assistance. The remainder of the air force was made up of 450 Ilyushin light bombers (range–1,000 miles) and possibly a small number of Russian Tu-4 heavy bombers.

The withdrawal of Soviet aid in 1960 resulted in a severe shortage of spare parts and aviation fuel. The numbers of available planes fell, and many were "cannibalised" to provide parts to keep the others flying. The quality of the pilots also fell due to shortage of fuel available for flying training. Only 2,000 planes were estimated to be capable of flying in 1964, but with the assignment of high priority to the air force, and the solving of the fuel shortage problem, the number of available planes has now increased to 2,500. Of these 2,500 aircraft, 2,000 are jet fighter interceptors, mostly MIG-17s, plus some MIG-19s and a handful of supersonic MIG-21s, which the Chinese may now have succeeded in producing themselves from prototypes supplied years before by the USSR. As regards bombers, the Chinese are thought to have only 200–300 remaining Ilyushins left, and to have opted to bypass the manned-bomber stage in favour of developing a missile capacity for their nuclear weapons.

Navy

China cannot be classed as a modern naval power. The total tonnage of the navy has never exceeded 200,000 tons, with the largest ships being four destroyers, and a similar number of destroyer escorts. The rest of the navy of several hundred vessels is composed of motor torpedo boats, frigates, minesweepers, patrol boats and gunboats. The navy also has 30 Soviet long-range class submarines (mostly built in China), at least one of which has been fitted with ballistic missile launching tubes capable of being fired while submerged.

These could be fitted with nuclear-tipped intermediate range missiles to give China a nuclear deterrent force.

Unable to operate far from its home bases (one of which, Port Arthur, was transferred by the Soviet Union back to China in 1955), and lacking any good amphibious capability, the Chinese navy is primarily a defensive force, designed for the protection of fishing fleets and coastal waters.

Functions of the armed forces

The primary functions of the PLA are to guard the state against external attack and internal rebellion. As article 20 of the PRC Constitution states: "the armed forces of the People's Republic of China belong to the people; their duty is to safeguard the gains of the people's revolution and the achievements of national construction, and to defend the sovereignty, territorial integrity and security of the state".

As a defence against possible attack, the majority of Chinese troops are deployed in border and coastal areas. In 1965 it was estimated that 200,000 men were stationed in southern China along the borders with North Vietnam; as many as three-quarters of a million in the coastal provinces opposite Taiwan; 200,000 in Tibet and along the frontier with India; 250,000 in Sinkiang; 250,000 in Manchuria close to the borders of the Soviet Union and North Korea; and the remainder distributed throughout the interior of the country. Since 1965, there has been some redeployment, with more troops being allocated to the Sinkiang and Manchurian areas, where there have been constant border clashes with the Soviet Union. Sinkiang is the site of China's nuclear weapons testing base, and Manchuria has a great deal of heavy industry. Both are considered to be of the highest strategic importance.

Few details are known about the positioning of the air force. Much of its strength is apparently concentrated, like the army, in border areas, near North Vietnam, on Hainan Island, in Tibet, and in Sinkiang and Manchuria. The navy operates out of four main bases, Dairen–Port Arthur on the Liaotung peninsula, Tsingtao in Shantung province, Shanghai and Canton.

In addition to external defence, the armed forces also guard against internal discontent. This reached considerable proportions during the years 1959–61, following the disasters the Great Leap, when peasant disaffection became widespread, and armed rebellions occurred. The deployment of large forces in the border areas is also designed to exert control over the national minority peoples, and to guard against any trends towards local autonomy in regions far from central control.

The task of maintaining law and order within the state rose to new prominence because of the disruption caused by the Cultural Revolution, and the increasing amount of conflict between various factional groups. This function was stressed in 1968 on the 41st anniversary of the PLA by the *Liberation Army Daily* of 31 July which described the army as a "strong force, not only for defence against aggression by external enemies, but also for preventing domestic enemies from usurping and subverting our proletarian political power".

In addition to its strictly military tasks, the PLA also performs a number of subsidiary functions in the sphere of production, administration and propaganda. The PLA had initially assumed a major role in production in 1949, but this was quickly terminated in most areas because of the Korean War. Production work by PLA men re-started after the cessation of hostilities, but only began on a large scale in 1956, when many troops were assigned to help the collectivisation campaign. Help given during this period was largely in the form of manpower, construction projects and technical aid. The amount of economic aid rendered by the PLA increased dramatically during the Great Leap Forward, and was orientated more towards industrial construction, water conservation and help with transportation. Following the Great Leap, the PLA helped with relief work in agriculture to cope with the floods and drought. However, this kind of activity fell off after 1963, and the PLA only helped out in the communes from time to time, and assisted with local public work projects.

There are several reasons why the Party insists that the PLA take part in economic work. First of all, such work is considered to be beneficial to the economy, and cements good relations between the civilians and the military. The PLA is also used to spearhead major economic and social reforms, with trained PLA cadres sent to the villages to organise and

...asants for land reform or communisation. ...labour is believed to strengthen the political ...standpoint of the PLA. However, overem- ...on non-military tasks has engendered opposition from within the PLA, some officers considering that this wasted valuable training time.

During the Cultural Revolution, the participation of the PLA in economic work again reached the high level attained during the Great Leap period. PLA men were heavily employed in agriculture, especially during the busy seasons. The PLA also set up and ran its own factories for many items, and PLA men were sent to other industrial enterprises to carry out Maoist propaganda work.

Finally, the PLA performs an administrative and propaganda function. The use of the PLA for administrative control purposes in communist China was started in 1949 in the newly liberated areas (although the military had had previous experience of administration before 1949) when Military Control Commissions were established for the interim period before a civilian government was organised. This period had come to an end by 1952, and the PLA did not play a major role in administration again until 1963-4, when, as part of the national emulation campaign to "Learn from the PLA", new Political Departments, modelled on the political control organs within the PLA, and under the command of the PLA, were established in all economic, industrial and governmental units. These Political Departments were staffed primarily by PLA cadres, and the military has become a model of behaviour for the civilian population, as well as a major source of recruitment for political training.

In 1967, with the Cultural Revolution in full spate, the earlier Military Control Commissions were revived, and set up in Peking, Kwangtung, and other cities and provinces. These Commissions exercised general authority within their areas, taking over control of the public security forces. The PLA also assumed responsibility for road, rail, and telephone traffic.

With the PLA acting as the chosen vehicle for the propagation throughout the country of the "Thought of Mao Tsetung", and with Mao being forced to rely more and more on the army to maintain order, the political influence of the military continued to rise. This was clearly reflected in the composition of the new Central Committee elected at the Ninth Party Congress, for of 279 full and alternate CC members, no fewer than 127 were PLA men.

PLA command structure and political control

At the head of the PLA chain of command is the Military Affairs Committee (MAC), a department of the CCP Central Committee. The MAC controls the Ministry of National Defence, under which is established the PLA General Headquarters. PLA General Headquarters is divided into three sections: the general staff department, general political department, and the general rear services (logistics) department. The country as a whole is divided into thirteen regional military commands, each in charge of two or more provinces and named after the city in which the command is headquartered, except for three military regions which command only one autonomous area each, and are named after that area—Inner Mongolia, Sinkiang and Tibet. The regional commands are subdivided into military district commands where the regional command covers two or more provinces, with the district commanding a single province. In addition there are also military garrison commands set up for major cities, and responsible either to the regional or district command.

Political control over the PLA was (at least up until the time of the Cultural Revolution) designed to implement Mao's dictum that "political power grows out of the barrel of a gun. Our principle is that the Party commands the gun, and the gun must never be allowed to command the Party".[4] At the head of the political control structure is the MAC, of which Mao Tse-tung is formally the Chairman, with Lin Piao (Minister of Defence) as the *de facto* head. The MAC, with guidance from the CCP Politburo, formulates military policy, and oversees its implementation through the network of Party committees within the PLA paralleling the military command structure. Party policy is passed down the Party

[4] *Selected Military Writings of Mao Tse-tung* (Peking: Foreign Language Press, 1966), p. 274.

chain of command to the Party branch at the company level, which is the basic unit of Party organisation in the PLA. It is the Party committee which is responsible for ensuring that the military obeys Party orders. Both the political commissar and the military commander of the unit will be members of the Party committee, with the commissar responsible for political affairs and the commander for military affairs.

The company political department is responsible for the political indoctrination of the troops, and is responsible to its superior political department, up to the general political department under the MAC.

The modernisation of the PLA began in 1951 during the Korean War. In addition to technical equipment, this also involved the introduction of conscription (although Chinese troops in Korea were formally designated as "volunteers"), a reorganisation of the chain of command, and the inauguration of a system of ranks and insignia for officers. With the process of modernisation of the armed forces, which incorporated many elements from the Soviet model, there was a decreased stress on political work, and increased emphasis on military expertise. However, from 1956 onwards, the Party reasserted the need for political controls over the military, and the need for political indoctrination of the officer corps. This naturally raised the stature of the political commissar within the military units, to the detriment of the military commander, who complained of too much time given to political work at the expense of military training. These complaints were reflected at the very highest levels, and were partially responsible for the dismissal of Marshal P'eng Teh-huai, Minister of National Defence, in 1959, and his replacement by Lin Piao. From 1960 onwards with the appointment of Lin Piao, the drive to inculcate a higher level of Party commitment on the part of the PLA was redoubled. One aspect of this work was the reconstruction of the Party apparatus within the PLA. In 1953 there were 1,200,000 Party members in the armed forces. By 1960, however, no Party branch committees could be found in one third of all PLA companies. This situation was quickly rectified, for the following year all companies that had lacked Party committees had re-established them, and 229,000 new Party members had been recruited from within the PLA. The leadership of the Party committee and the political commissar within the military unit was stressed, and those officers who questioned the military competence of the commissars were denounced by the CCP. New regulations published in 1963 further elevated the status of the political commissar vis-à-vis the military commander, and with "politics in command", the commissar became the dominant partner.

In 1965 the PLA chose to re-emphasise its egalitarian and democratic characteristics by abolishing the system of ranks, insignia and awards for officers that had been in force since 1955, therefore deviating again from the Soviet model and reverting to the revolutionary tradition of former times.

The PLA and the Cultural Revolution

In the years immediately before the Cultural Revolution the movement to place "politics in command" within the PLA came to refer specifically to "Mao-study". The PLA became a forerunner in distributing to all troops copies of Mao's *Selected Readings* and the ubiquitous little red book of *Quotations*. By 1966, therefore, the PLA had become a model for the study of the "Thoughts of Mao Tse-tung", and a suitable object for imitation by people, government and Party.

However, the giving of pre-eminence to politics within the PLA tended to generate its own counter-current in the form of opposition from those who thought that too little weight was being given to military factors. This position was pithily summed up by P'eng Teh-huai, who was reported to have said (before his dismissal in 1959): "What's the use of relying entirely on political and ideological work? It can't fly. . . ."[5] This comment typified the views of many senior officers, who felt that although political work was important, even vital, and should be given equal weight with military work, nevertheless, military and technological considerations should not be made subordinate to political ends.

Mao and Lin Piao were adamant in stressing the primacy

[5] *New China News Agency,* 30 August 1967.

of political work, and the resulting tensions within the PLA produced a spate of dismissals within the military. One of the first of these was the Chief of Staff, Lo Jui-ch'ing, who disappeared from view in late 1965. He was later criticised for having opposed the Cultural Revolution and Maoist policies with his "bourgeois military line", which gave more importance in warfare to the effects of weapons and technique, and less to the human factor and to the "spiritual atom-bomb" of Mao Tse-tung's Thought. Lo Jui-ch'ing was linked in his deviations to former Minister of Defence P'eng Teh-huai, who was accused of wanting to de-escalate the quarrel with the USSR because he felt the need for Soviet assistance to China in the field of modern weapons and nuclear arms. The Maoists, however, downgraded the value of technique and nuclear weapons, and placed emphasis on the revolutionary purity of the CCP as compared with the revisionism of the Soviet leaders, and therefore opted for self-reliance on the part of China, and concentrated on political indoctrination rather than technical proficiency in the armed forces. Another clue to Lo's dismissal was the re-introduction of large-scale economic work, particularly in agriculture, to be done by the PLA during the Cultural Revolution. P'eng Teh-huai had apparently opposed the excessive use of the army for this purpose during the Great Leap Forward, and no doubt the professionals felt the same way in 1966-7.

Initially, the responsibility for the execution of the Cultural Revolution within the PLA was left in the hands of the PLA General Political Department, rather than being given to the Central Committee's Cultural Revolution Group. The 8 August 1966 decision of the CCP Central Committee stated that the Cultural Revolution in the armed forces "should be carried out in accordance with the instructions of the Military Commission of the Central Committee of the Party and the General Political Department of the PLA". A PLA Cultural Revolution Group was also established under the leadership of a deputy-director of the General Political Department, but these arrangements did not work well, for in January 1967, the PLA's Cultural Revolution Group was put under the command of Hsü Hsiang-ch'ien, a former PLA Marshal, and the Group was placed under the control of the CCP Central

Committee Cultural Revolution Group and Military Affairs Committee.

Chiang Ch'ing was made adviser to the new Group. However, this arrangement proved to be no better than the one before. In April 1967, Hsü Hsiang-ch'ien was replaced by Hsiao Hua, Director of the PLA General Political Department, Yang Ch'eng-wu, Lo Jui-ch'ing's replacement as Chief of Staff (and himself dismissed in March 1968), and Hsieh Fu-chih, the Public Security Minister. Even so, stability was not to be achieved, for Hsiao Hua came under severe criticism and fell later that year. With his fall, the PLA General Political Department ceased to function.

Nuclear weapons development

The Chinese programme to develop and test nuclear weapons probably began in the early 1950s, with the help of extensive aid from the Soviet Union. Under a 1957 agreement between the two countries, the USSR supplied China with an experimental nuclear reactor, and Chinese atomic scientists were trained in the Soviet Union. At the same time, the Russians agreed to provide a sample atomic bomb, together with technical details concerning its manufacture. However, the Russians reneged on their promise in 1959, and their help with the Chinese nuclear programme came to a virtual halt. The Russians also urged China not to become a nuclear power. The Chinese, believing that they could no longer be guaranteed the protection of the Soviet nuclear "umbrella", aimed at a policy of self-reliance by making their own weapons, and, by making faster progress than had been expected, were able to detonate their first "device" on 16 October 1964. The bomb was equivalent to 20,000 tons of TNT, and was detonated at the main testing site of Lop Nor in Sinkiang. Analysis of the fallout from the bomb showed that it had contained enriched uranium, not plutonium, indicating that the Chinese were technologically more advanced in this field than had been estimated. The production of enriched uranium (by a gaseous diffusion plant near Lanchow in Kansu, north-west China), showed that priority was being given to the development of fusion (hydrogen) weapons.

A second bomb, similar to the first, was exploded in 1965.

The third explosion of May 1966 was stated to have contained "thermonuclear materials", and on 17 June 1967, China exploded its first hydrogen bomb, equivalent to three megatons, in the Lop Nor area. A second hydrogen bomb was tested in December 1968, and a third on 29 September 1969. The first underground test took place on 23 September 1969.

Possessing the ability to produce nuclear weapons in limited quantities, the Chinese have been giving top priority to the development of a delivery system, and have abandoned the manned-bomber stage in favour of concentrating on missile delivery. The test explosion of an atomic bomb in October 1966 was stated to have been a "guided missile nuclear weapon". A missile testing range exists in Sinkiang, and it is thought by some Western experts that China has already tested an intermediate range missile (1,500 miles range), and will complete an intercontinental ballistic missile within the near future. China is also working towards the operation of ballistic missile submarines, and is known to have one such submarine at present.

Overall direction of the nuclear programme is the responsibility of Nieh Jung-chen, Chairman of the Scientific and Technological Commission of the State Council, and a member of the Central Committee. During the Cultural Revolution there were signs that the influence of the PLA over the programme had increased. The missile research programme is headed by Ch'ien Hsüeh-sen, an American-trained physicist who returned to China in 1955 after nearly twenty years in the United States.

The Chinese, like the Russians, believe that the "socialist camp" is now sufficiently strong to deter the West from an all-out attack. The Chinese do not, therefore, believe that nuclear war is inevitable. Where they differ from the Russians is in their assessment of the dangers of a nuclear war arising out of a local conflict, or war of "national liberation". The Chinese tend to discount the dangers of this happening, and claim that the Russians overemphasise the risks in order to excuse themselves from giving more aid to revolutionary movements. The Chinese feel that since new communist regimes are unlikely to be set up except by violence, refusal to help and support wars of national liberation is tantamount to abandoning the spread of the revolution.

Far more than accidental war, what the Chinese fear is a deliberate first strike launched against them by the USA, or even by the USA and the USSR acting together. For this reason they have devoted many valuable resources to building up a stock of weapons and developing a delivery system, so as to be able to deter a nuclear strike against them by the threat of at least limited retaliation.

The immediate causes of an American attack could be a crisis over Taiwan, or result from the Vietnam War, and the Chinese envisage either a limited strike on their nuclear installations, or a larger attack designed to destroy major urban, industrial and communication centres. For this reason, they have stressed the need to evacuate people from crowded areas, to build factories and military installations in places far from concentrations of population, and the development of a people's militia to assist the regular armed forces. The Chinese believe that even if they suffered heavy damage to their industry and cities, because of their vast territory and immense population, communism of the primitive Yenan-type would continue, and that the Americans would be forced to invade the country physically with troops, at which point they would eventually be defeated by a protracted guerrilla war, similar to that employed against the Japanese.

In addition to possessing a credible deterrent against a possible US (or Soviet) attack, the Chinese also perceive that their possession of nuclear weapons will gain them increased influence, particularly in South-east Asia, where nuclear blackmail could be employed to reassert Chinese hegemony in the area.

The Chinese have stated many times, however, that they will never be the first to use nuclear weapons. Certainly it is unlikely that they would do so against either of the two superpowers, or a third country protected by treaty with the USA or USSR, because of the massive retaliation that could be expected.

The Chinese have refused to sign the tri-partite partial Test Ban Treaty of 1963, and have attacked the Non-Proliferation Treaty adopted by the United Nations in June 1968. These moves are viewed as further evidence of Soviet-American collusion to deprive other countries of nuclear weapons, and so increase their world domination. The more countries have the bomb, says China, the more the Americans will be deterred from using it, and the less the chances of a nuclear war. The Chinese have put forward their own proposals for disarmament, which advocate the mutual destruction of nuclear weapons by all countries. Since China would lose little by this, compared with the United States or the Soviet Union, but would be left with very large conventional forces, these proposals are unlikely to be accepted.

The militia

The militia is designed to play a key role in the defensive strategy China aims to employ following a possible nuclear strike against her territory. Theoretically a purely volunteer force, whose members are differentiated from the PLA because they do not cease their normal occupations, the militia is envisaged as a weapon of great value in assisting the regular forces of the PLA to ward off an enemy invasion. In addition to their wartime role, the militia routinely helps maintain law and order in the rural areas, and works with the public security service.

After a temporary expansion of the militia during the Korean War, when it acted as a reservoir of trained recruits for the PLA, its role declined until it was revivified by the Great Leap Forward of 1958, and the accompanying campaign to make "Everyone a Soldier". From an estimated twenty-two million in 1953, the strength of the militia rose to over 220 million during the Great Leap. This reflected the increasing militarisation of society at that time. A second factor instrumental in expanding the militia force in 1958–9 was the widening gulf between China and the Soviet Union, creating an awareness in China that the Russians would not help China with nuclear weapons production, and that China could not be guaranteed protection under the Soviet nuclear shield. The Chinese leaders therefore saw the country as being extremely vulnerable to nuclear attack, and reasoned that the defensive strategy of a "people's war" would provide the most effective deterrent. "People's war" is based on the assumption that the enemy would be forced to invade the country with land forces, in which they would become bogged down with over-extended lines of communication, and eventually defeated by a politically motivated population, carrying out guerrilla warfare, and backed by the regular and militia forces numbering hundreds of millions in all. This strategy would be employed against either an American or Russian invasion.

During the Great Leap, the militia was organised into two categories, basic and ordinary. The basic militia contained only the younger, able-bodied citizens, aged from eighteen to thirty, and was the only category to possess arms, the ordinary militia was much larger, contained a higher proportion of older people, and was not issued with rifles. With the deteriorating situation in the countryside from 1959 onwards, much of the militia organisation in many areas fell into abeyance, so that only the basic militia was active, and receiving any training. Militia organisation has been revitalised since 1964, with its numbers stabilised at a much smaller figure of ten million, of which most are demobilised PLA men.

However, although the militia has declined in numbers since the Great Leap (but improved in quality), there has been no diminution in the policy of "self-reliance", and its corollary of an independent nuclear capability and reliance on "people's war" to deter a hostile invasion. Within the framework of "people's war", the militia continues to play a key role.

The concept of "people's war" is based on the Maoist belief in the dominance of human will and politics over technical superiority in weapons. The Maoist leadership therefore places great stress on the political and ideological arming of the population in preparation for a possible enemy invasion. Mao believes that in this kind of war, the enemy, although superior in armaments, will eventually be defeated by a protracted war of attrition, as he lured deep into the country, and ensnared in a net composed of the regular forces, the militia, and a politically conscious, aroused and hostile native population.

Consequently, it is argued by the Chinese that "to concentrate our troops to annihilate powerful attacking enemy forces, we must adopt the policy of luring them in deep and abandon some cities and districts of our own accord in a planned way, so as to let them in. It is only after letting the enemy in that the people can take part in the war in various ways and that the power of a people's war can be fully exerted. It is only after letting the enemy in that he can be compelled to divide up his forces, take on heavy burdens and commit mistakes. In other words, we must let the enemy become elated, stretch out all his ten fingers and become hopelessly bogged down. Thus, we can concentrate superior forces to destroy the enemy forces one by one, to eat them up mouthful by mouthful".[6] In Maoist terminology the enemy is "despised" strategically (i.e. in the long run) as only a "paper tiger", but tactically (in the short run) the enemy must be seen as dangerous, and defeated by isolating small units and attacking them with overwhelming numbers. Therefore, "concentrating a superior force to destroy the enemy forces one by one is the materialisation in military affairs of Comrade Mao Tse-tung's strategic and tactical thinking of strategically 'pitting one against ten' and tactically 'pitting ten against one'."[7]

At least since the time of the Great Leap, there has been a continuing history of opposition from within both the PLA and the Party to Maoist military policies. This opposition has usually been identified with P'eng Teh-huai (purged in 1959), and more recently with Lo Jui-ch'ing and Liu Shao-ch'i (amongst others) both of whom were removed from their positions during the Cultural Revolution.

In general, the criticisms have been centred not on any demands to abolish Party control over the military, but on the need to give at least equal weight to military factors, such as the need for military training, and advanced weapons, and to ensure that the demands of political indoctrination do not come in the way of the armed forces' capacity to fight.

Specifically, P'eng Teh-huai is alleged to have favoured a *rapprochement* with the USSR during the Great Leap, rather than an ideological confrontation with the Soviet Union,

[6] Li Tso-peng, *Strategy: One Against Ten. Tactics: Ten Against One* (Peking: Foreign Languages Press, 1966), pp. 23–4.
[7] ibid., pp. 39–40.

which would deprive China of technical assistance and the protection of the Soviet nuclear umbrella. Related criticisms came from the fact that Mao's policies logically led to a re-vitalisation of the concept of "people's war", and an increased role for the militia.

The opposition to Mao's policies charged that the doctrine of "people's war" was old-fashioned, and no longer the most suitable defence in a nuclear era. They also objected to the growth of the civilian militia and the "Everyone a Soldier" campaign, claiming that larger and more modernised regular forces would be more efficient. Rather than stress the ideo-logical indoctrination of the population, they proposed to give equal weight to the need for modern weapons and adequate training. They also opposed the tactics of "people's war" on the grounds that "luring the enemy in deep" in order to de-stroy him would result in tremendous damage to the country, and preferred to adopt a policy of using the PLA to engage the invaders "beyond the gates" on the frontiers of China.

Although the Cultural Revolution purge has curbed the ex-pression of such views, there is no doubt that they will con-tinue to find some favour within both the Party and the PLA.

However, given the fact that China does not as yet possess an effective nuclear delivery system with which to deter at-tack from either the USA or the USSR, the overall strategy of "people's war", with its demand for a large militia, not only acts as a morale booster for the civilian population, but also makes the best use of China's available defences of vast ter-ritory and population against the possibility of a nuclear or conventional invasion.

5

ECONOMIC AND SOCIAL POLICIES

Period of consolidation and reconstruction 1949–52

There were a number of factors basic to the Chinese economy which the communist planners were forced to take into account on their assumption of control over the mainland in 1949. For example, it was estimated that at that time, the population stood at approximately 540 million. The Chinese claimed that large numbers were an asset, and although a big population could be considered desirable for the labour-intensive cultivation of an underdeveloped country, it was also the case that this population was expanding at some 2 per cent per annum (i.e. fourteen to fifteen million more people per year), so that output needed to expand annually by this amount just to maintain existing standards, without regard to any improvement in the lot of the people. Furthermore, although China had a land area slightly larger than that of the USA, only about 15 per cent of it was cultivated. Since few people lived in cities, this meant a very high density of population in good agricultural areas, with high yields per acre, but low yields per man.

Because the peasants were living at subsistence level, there was little saving, and few funds available for investment in industrialisation. This situation could only be improved by the use of new farming practices, new technology and mechanisation, or by improved organisation. The CCP was to choose the last option.

With respect to other resources, however, China was more favourably situated. Coal and water power were abundant, and oil and iron-ore reserves were reasonably good. Although the natural resources present were more than ample to sustain a modern industrial economy, the problem in China's case was that the development and exploitation of these resources, such as the transformation of coal and water power into energy, required a heavy investment in capital equipment.

Given these relatively fixed economic variables such as population, land and other natural resources, the policy of the communist planners in 1949 was initially to make good use of the first period of peace the country had experienced for twelve years so as to restore industrial and agricultural production to its pre-war levels, bring about a measure of financial stability by curbing the rampant inflation, and to rebuild the transport network. From then on, the broad outline of economic development was to follow that of the Soviet Union, towards agricultural collectivisation, industrialisation and the abolition of private enterprise, and economic relations were to be oriented away from the West and towards the Soviet bloc. In these initial aims, the CCP was very successful. Although the first period of land redistribution resulted in smaller farms than before, overall, economic production rose throughout the 1949–52 period, so that by 1952 it was back to pre-war levels. In addition, inflation had been curtailed, the rail network was largely restored, and new construction started. Much of the recovery was due to the mildness of the treatment of private capitalists, who continued in most areas to run their own enterprises with only a modicum of state control. The CCP had, however, gained experience of large-scale planning in Manchuria (the most industrially developed area) and knowledge of running industrial plants throughout the mainland, which was to stand them in good stead in the forthcoming Five Year Plan.

Agricultural policies 1949–57

Having gone much of the way towards restoring agricultural production in 1949, the CCP embarked on a nation-wide policy of land redistribution. This policy had already been implemented in some of the areas controlled by the communists before 1949, but was extended to cover the whole country with the promulgation of the Agrarian Reform Law of June 1950. The land redistribution was carried out area by area, with Party cadres first dividing up the rural population according to their class status.

Broadly speaking, there were five classes; landlords (who

owned land, but did not engage in labour), rich peasants (who owned land and employed labour but also worked their land themselves), middle peasants (who might own land, but depended mainly on their own labour to make a living), poor peasants (who usually rented land from others and hired out their labour-power), and farm labourers (who depended almost entirely on the sale of their labour-power for a living). It naturally made a great deal of difference to one's future life as to which category one was placed in, and there was considerable confusion because of variation in the criteria for differentiation applied in different areas. The land, animals, tools and other property of the landlords were expropriated, as was much of the land and property of the rich peasants. This confiscated land and property were then distributed to the poor and landless peasants, while the property of the middle peasants was protected.

Land redistribution was a first step towards improving agricultural productivity, but its prime motive was political, to break the power of the landlord class. Speaking on the Agrarian Reform Law in June 1950, Liu Shao-ch'i said:

The basic reason for and the aim of agrarian reform are different from the view that agrarian reform is only designed to relieve the poor people. The Communist Party has always been fighting for the interests of the labouring poor, but the viewpoint of communists has always been different from that of the philanthropists. The results of agrarian reform are beneficial to the impoverished labouring peasants, helping the peasants partly solve their problem of poverty. *But the basic aim of agrarian reform is not merely one of relieving the poor peasants. It is designed to free the rural productive forces from the shackles of the feudal land ownership system of the landlord class, in order to develop agricultural production and thus pave the way for New China's industrialisation.*[1]

Although in some parts, the landlords attempted to give their land over to the peasants voluntarily, the Party prohibited this, and forced the landlords to attend mass trials, at which, urged on by the cadres, the peasants accused them of past misdeeds. Many landlords were executed after the trials,

[1] Liu Shao-ch'i speaking to the National Committee of the CPPCC on 14 June 1950 (my italics).

the figures probably running into the millions. Politically, therefore, land redistribution was a success, for the power of the landlords and gentry, both political and economic, was broken, and much goodwill was won from the rest of the rural population through the distribution of their confiscated land, farm animals and tools. Economically, land reform was less successful. The redistribution of former estates led to a decline in area of the average holding, and to no increase in productivity. Therefore in order to increase production and facilitate centralised planning, the CCP at the same time as carrying out the land redistribution (which was largely completed by 1952) worked out plans for eventual collectivisation of the land.

The first step on the road to collectivisation was the formation of mutual-aid teams. Initially, these were based on a practice which was traditional in China of pooling resources to compensate for shortages of labour, draught animals and tools during the busy seasons of sowing and harvesting. These seasonal mutual aid teams comprised from three to five households on average, and sprung into existence only during the busy seasons. Gradually, they were converted into permanent mutual aid teams of six to ten households, in which communal use was made of resources, while the peasants retained private ownership of their land, animals and farm implements. Income was based on the amount of land, etc., put into the team, plus the amount of work done.

The next step was the formation of agricultural producers' cooperatives (APCs). These had been introduced as early as 1952, but the decision to move from the mutual aid team to the APC was only taken in late 1953. Each APC had approximately forty households in it; there was further division of labour; and land use, labour and animals were subject to collective management. However, the peasants still retained, at least in theory, the ownership of their land, and could opt out of the cooperative at will. Since private ownership of land still existed, the APCs were only semi-socialist in character, and income was received according to the inputs of land and labour. Poor crop yields in the early years of the first Five Year Plan (1953–7), plus the lack of economic incentives and manufactured goods for sale in the countryside caused the peasants to raise their own consumption and reduce the surplus available to the state, which led to a speeding up of the process of collectivisation as from the autumn of 1955.

It was hoped that the formation of "advanced" APCs would lead to a big increase in agricultural production, which was vital if the targets of the first Five Year Plan were to be fulfilled. Industrial crops from the agricultural sector of the economy, such as cotton, provided as much as 90 per cent of the raw materials for light industry, as well as three-quarters of the exports needed to finance imports of equipment required for industrialisation. In the advanced or higher APCs, land was owned collectively, and the peasants received no income from it, but were paid a wage on the basis of their work performed on the collective. Each peasant was allowed to maintain a small private plot on which he could raise vegetables or chickens. By mid-1956, more than 90 per cent of all peasant households had joined the APCs, and most of these were of the advanced type, so that by the end of the year, less than 5 per cent of the land remained in private hands. Although there was considerable slaughter of draught cattle, agriculture had been collectivised in China with much less terror and hostile reactions from the peasants than had been the case in the Soviet Union.

During the 1949–57 period, the main emphasis was on getting bigger yields from the existing acreage, partially by means of improved irrigation, with millions of peasants engaged in water conservation projects. Several million acres of previously uncultivated land were also reclaimed. However, the state investment in agriculture amounted to only 10 per cent of total state investment at most, and this proved to be insufficient to meet planned agricultural targets, in spite of the agricultural reorganisation. Targets of grain were not met, and cotton was always is short supply, leading to a rationing of cotton cloth, the operating of the textile industry below full capacity, and the need to import cotton.

Industrial policies 1949–57

As was the case with their policies towards agriculture, the communists were forced to adopt a moderate policy towards industry in the early years of their regime. Emerging from the countryside into the cities where they lacked a mass backing, they had to treat the managerial, commercial and technical personnel favourably in order to maintain the momentum of the economy. Initially, therefore, most enterprises were left in private hands, and the state nationalised only those concerns which had been owned by the KMT, which gave the CCP control over the railways, communications and the banking and financial sectors. According to article 10 of the state Constitution, "the policy of the state towards capitalist industry and commerce is to use, restrict and transform them". The period of "use" lasted from 1949 to 1951, during which time private industry played a dominant role, and helped rejuvenate the economy. The period of "restriction" lasted from 1952 to 1953, with the government limiting private enterprise with respect to sales, profits, and production. Restriction was also facilitated by the Party-directed "five-anti" campaign of early 1952. This campaign was launched against the urban bourgeoisie, who were accused of bribery, tax evasion, theft of state property and of state economic secrets, and cheating on government contracts. Industrialists, merchants and businessmen were denounced at public trials reminiscent of the land reform movement in the countryside. Many committed suicide or were executed, and others were luckier to escape with a fine or a period in a corrective labour camp. Overall, the five-anti campaign succeeded in reducing both the economic and political power of the capitalists.

The period of "transformation" 1954–7, was divided into two stages. First of all, emphasis was placed on the gradual transformation of private enterprises into joint state–private enterprises, with the operations of the plant directed by the state, and production integrated into the national plan. Owners and investors in the plant were given interest payments of 5 per cent per annum on their investment. This programme was accelerated rapidly in the latter half of 1955 and early 1956 with the second stage of development known as joint operation by whole trades. With this second stage, 90 per cent of all un-socialised industry was brought into joint state–private management, so that by 1956 not only had agriculture been collectivised, but industry had been brought under virtually complete state control, and with a minimised disruption, owing to the state's policy of "buying off" the capitalists with interest payments.

The first Five Year Plan began in 1953, following the truce in Korea and agreement on Soviet economic aid, and terminated in 1957. However, it was not publicly announced until mid-1955, and for the first two and a half years the Chinese operated on the basis of annual plans. It was estimated at that time by Mao Tse-tung that three Five Year Plans would be required for the construction of a socialist society, and forty or fifty years "to build a powerful country with a high degree of socialist industrialisation".

The Chinese plan was based on the Soviet model of economic development, namely the concentration of resources on the construction of a heavy industrial base, and the relative neglect of light industry (consumer goods) and agriculture. The investment for the heavy industrial base (capital goods and raw materials industries) was to come from the agricultural surplus provided by collectivisation. During 1953–7, therefore, of the total state investment, 56 per cent went to industry (87 per cent of this for heavy industry and only 13 per cent for light), 18.7 per cent into transport and communications, and only 8.2 per cent for agriculture, forestry and water conservation.[2]

Considerable progress was registered in heavy industrial development during the first Five Year Plan period, especially in iron and steel production, as well as fuels (except for petroleum), raw materials, electric power and the machine tool industry. Trucks, cars, jet aircraft and ships were produced for the first time. From 1952 to 1957 the average annual rate of growth of industrial production was between 14–19 per cent.[3] New roads were built which were of military and political as well as economic value, for instance to Tibet, and there was further railroad construction. A second line to the Soviet Union was opened, via Outer Mongolia, and a third was under construction through Sinkiang (which has yet to be completed).

[2] Choh-ming Li, "Economic Development", *China Quarterly*, no. 1 (January–March 1960), p. 40.
[3] Alexander Eckstein, *Communist China's Economic Growth and Foreign Trade* (New York: McGraw-Hill, 1966), p. 48.

Reflecting the scale of priorities during the Plan, neither light industry nor agriculture performed so well. The relative neglect of agricultural investment meant that agricultural production only increased by an annual average of 4.5 per cent from 1952 to 1957. One reason for this failure was the worsening ratio of population to land, for while the land acreage increased by only 3 per cent over the period, population rose 10 per cent. Another reason was the failure of the ideologically correct policy of collectivisation significantly to raise agricultural productivity. The planners therefore overestimated the benefits of collectivisation, and tended to underestimate the effect of agricultural performance on industrial production. It was no accident that industrial production was low in 1954 and 1955, following the poor harvests of 1953 and 1954, and that high industrial output followed a year after good crops. Poor annual increases in food grains meant fewer food exports (since the increase in food grains only just kept ahead of the population increase), and this led to reduced imports of industrial equipment. Furthermore, agriculture was relied upon to provide many of the raw materials for light industry, such as cotton, tobacco and sugar. Therefore, fluctuations in agriculture resulted in fluctuations in industry.

Although it was becoming increasingly clear by the end of the Plan that agriculture was a stumbling block, the Plan as a whole was a success, for Western economists estimated that China's gross national product rose 6–9 per cent per annum during the 1953–7 Plan period, and even the lowest figure was about three times the annual increase of population. Virtually all the investment, which had produced industrial expansion surpassed only by Pakistan and Japan, had been made from internal savings, and it is in this context that the effect of Soviet aid on the Chinese economy must be evaluated.

The Soviet Union supplied only two loans for Chinese economic development, one of US$300 million in 1950, and a second of US$130 million in 1953. Both were loans, rather than gifts, and were repaid with interest. These loans went towards paying for the 211 complete industrial plants which the Russians (by 1956) had agreed to construct. Not all of these plants were completed during the Plan period. Although these Soviet loans totalled only 3 per cent of all state investment during 1953–7, the complete plants provided by the Russians became the core of China's heavy industrial base, since they were mainly steel and machine tool factories, tractor works, chemical, plastics and petroleum projects and railroad construction, as well as computers and a nuclear reactor. Repayment of the first loan began in 1954, and China's export surplus in her trade with the USSR grew from 1956 as she continued to repay the loans, plus an unspecified sum for Soviet military equipment supplied during the Korean War.

However, the Russians supplied additional invaluable aid in the form of blueprints and an estimated 10,000 experts and technicians (plus 1,500 from Eastern Europe) who worked on the projects at one time or another and also advised on the reorganisation of finance, taxation, planning and management. Furthermore, by 1957, some 7,000 Chinese students had studied in the USSR, and a similar number of workers had gained experience in Soviet factories and offices.

The Great Leap Forward

Although industry, and particularly heavy industry, had expanded rapidly during the first Five Year Plan, agriculture had not responded nearly as well, and it was becoming clear in the latter stages of the Plan that a bottleneck existed in the agricultural sector, for not only did this sector supply most of the food for home consumption, but also a major part of the raw materials for light industry, exports with which to pay for industrial imports, and a sizable proportion of the savings for new capital investment. The problem was therefore one of concurrently expanding agriculture and industry, of preventing agricultural stagnation and continuing the industrial progress achieved under the Plan. The first move in this new development strategy of "walking with two legs" was designed to make use of the surplus of rural labour while overcoming the chronic shortage of capital.

Vast water conservation and irrigation projects were organised in the winter of 1957–8, mobilising 100 million people on a scale not attempted before. These projects quickly soaked up the surplus labour, and actually created a shortage, which was aggravated by the introduction of a campaign to build small-scale native industries in the rural areas in the spring of 1958, on which sixty million men were working. Clearly the collectives were too small a unit of organisation to administer these vast numbers, and furthermore, the shortage of labour required a change in rural organisation to permit women to be used in the fields. This was the basis on which the communes were to be developed.

The first model commune made its appearance in Honan in April 1958. From then on they spread rapidly over the mainland, so that by September there were 24,000 communes, each formed from the amalgamation of approximately thirty collectives and comprising 4,000–5,000 peasant households. Over 90 per cent of all peasant households were in the communes.

Whereas the collectives confined themselves to agricultural functions, the communes combined industry and agriculture as well as education and military affairs, with the commune merging with the *hsiang* unit of local government. Each commune was divided up into production brigades, equivalent to the former advanced APCs (collectives), and production teams (equivalent to the former APCs), but with the commune as the real locus of economic decision making. The peasants' private plots were taken away, and much other property was collectivised. Collectivisation of life became the ultimate aim, as the peasants ate in communal mess halls, and were paid on a part-wage, part-supply basis whereby some wages were supplied in kind, in partial fulfilment of the communist principle of "to each according to his need".

A basic aim of the communes was to provide increased investment funds for the state, by making use of economies of scale, and obtaining greater output by improved rural organisation. By the use of communal mess halls, nurseries and homes for old people, women were "liberated" from household chores to work in the fields.

Grandiose claims were made for the success of the communes. In 1958 it was stated that China would catch up with and surpass Great Britain in the absolute output of major industrial items within fifteen years. Planned targets were continually raised during 1958, and it was claimed that they had been achieved by the end of the year. In April 1959 it was announced that food crops and iron and steel production had doubled during 1958.

However, by August 1959 the CCP was forced to downgrade its claims drastically, and agriculture and industry went into a steep decline for several years.

The factors contributing to the failure of the communes were many. A major factor was the hearty dislike of the peasant for the new communal living and eating arrangements, not to mention the endless exhortations to work harder. The CCP underestimated the value of material incentives, and with the removal of the private plots, and the downgrading of family life, the peasants' morale fell, they worked lethargically, slaughtered farm animals, and productivity plummeted. The hastily built water conservation and irrigation projects of winter 1957–8 proved to have been constructed without prior geological exploration, and in consequence millions of acres were turned into alkaline land or otherwise rendered unfit for cultivation. The statistical system collapsed under the pressure to ignore reality and inflate the figures, and made coherent planning impossible.

The "backyard" blast furnaces produced millions of tons of pig iron, but most of this was of such low quality as to be useless, but nevertheless the railroads were tied up in transporting it from the rural areas to the industrial centres. Industrial enterprises, trying to meet impossible quotas, overused their equipment by omitting regular maintenance, with the result that the machines eventually broke down—often irreparably, as spare part production had also largely been discontinued.

In December 1958 some of the rights to personal property were restored together with other incentives, and twelve hours a day for eating and resting were guaranteed. Further concessions were made in April 1959 when the peasants' small private plots of land were returned to them. In August of that year, the commune continued to shrink in importance, as many of its functions were devolved to the production brigade. This process was continued, when in January 1961 the commune was further decentralised to the level of the production team (the former APC), and the communal mess halls were abandoned. The communes did retain various local government functions and continued to manage some small industrial and water conservation projects.

The agricultural collapse naturally had serious effects on industry. The shortage of raw materials, particularly cotton and tobacco, led to a contraction of the light industrial sector, so that by 1961, 50 per cent of all light industrial plants had ceased production. This resulted in serious urban unemployment. New investment had to be curtailed, and foreign exchange reserves used to buy grain from the West, rather than for the purchase of industrial equipment. This situation was exacerbated by the increasing bitterness of the Sino–Soviet dispute,[4] leading to the precipitate withdrawal of all Soviet advisers and technicians from China in the summer of 1960 (1,390 at that time), taking their blueprints with them, and causing the halting of construction on many half-completed projects.

Agricultural production was very high in 1958, the first year of the Great Leap, owing to extremely good weather conditions. From then on, however, due to the factors above, plus bad weather, it fell rapidly until 1960; the recovery in food grains beginning in 1962, and cotton production only picking up in 1963. Steel production also fell from 1959 onwards, and only started to recover in 1962. Overall, therefore, the economy endured a "leap backward" from 1958 to 1961, started to recover in 1962, and by 1965 had reattained the level it had reached seven years earlier in 1958.

China's economic development strategy up to 1958 had followed the Soviet model of stress on heavy industry. The second Five Year Plan (1958–62), which was overtaken by the Great Leap, continued the emphasis on heavy industry and modern techniques, but added to it a policy of developing small-scale native industry, using indigenous methods and labour intensive techniques. This was the "walking with two legs" policy, which was taken a step further in January 1961, when, following the poor harvest of 1960, the Ninth Plenum of the Central Committee reduced investment in heavy industry. In contrast to the ecstatic enthusiasm of former years, the new policy was one of caution and gradualism. Li Fu-

[4] See Chapter 6.

ch'un admitted deficiencies in agricultural output and announced the end of the Great Leap, and a new policy of concentrating on the agricultural sector. At the same time the influence of the professionals and managers rose, as they were needed to rehabilitate the economy, and that of the radical ideologues fell. The change of economic policy was made final by the Tenth CC Plenum of September 1962, which spoke of "agriculture as the foundation of the national economy". In so doing, the Chinese continued their deviation (begun in 1958) from the Soviet model of economic development.

Third Five Year Plan and Cultural Revolution

Few reliable statistics have been issued since the aftermath of the Great Leap Forward. Nevertheless, the broad trends of economic strategy can be ascertained. From 1962 onwards, the chief aim was to rejuvenate the economy, while not allowing the capitalist tendencies in peasant agriculture to become too strong. Much stress was put on the expansion of the irrigated area, the use of industry for rural mechanisation and electrification, and the use of more chemical fertiliser. The birth control campaign, temporarily halted by the labour shortages of the Great Leap, was also revived in 1962.

China continued to import food grains from the West, mainly Australia and Canada, at a rate of five million tons per year. The bulk of China's international trade was now done with countries outside the Soviet bloc, a trend which accelerated once the final instalment of the debt to the USSR was paid in 1964. By 1966, the gross national output was probably about 30 per cent higher than that of 1957, most of the increase being due to industry, with agriculture only slightly above pre-Great Leap levels. Population may well have increased by some 100 million during the same period.

By this time, it was felt that the economy had recovered sufficiently to inaugurate the third Five Year Plan in 1966. The basic policy of giving priority to agriculture while proceeding with the gradual development of industry, was unchanged. "Self-reliance" was a keynote, and the effects of the emerging Cultural Revolution could be seen in the admonitions to "hold aloft the great Red Banner of Mao Tse-tung's

Thought" in the urging to "learn from the People's Liberation Army" and to "put ideological and political work first". China continued imports not only of grain, but also of complete plants from Western Europe and Japan, mainly in the chemical fertilisers, plastics and synthetic-fibre fields.

With the onset of the Cultural Revolution, the third Five Year Plan was discarded, as economic planning became impossible. Agriculture seemed to suffer relatively little from the effects of the political chaos, although there were reports of shortages of chemical fertiliser caused by the disruption of industrial production. Industry as a whole was only affected by serious if temporary disruptions after the Red Guards were formed in late 1966 and the workers joined in the Cultural Revolution early the following year. With the disruption of transport caused by Red Guards travelling the country "exchanging revolutionary experiences" and the eruption of factional violence, factories suffered from shortages of raw materials, and difficulty in shipping out their finished products. Both coal and oil production were down considerably in 1967 over 1966 figures. An even greater threat to future progress was represented by the demoralisation and downgrading of the professionals, managers and technicians, a major component in economic development, to which must be added the loss of two full years' education for millions of students.

Even though the Cultural Revolution was basically concluded by 1969, its effects on future economic growth are liable to make themselves felt for some time to come.

Educational policy

As with all communist party-states, China seeks not passive acquiescence on the part of citizens to the demands of the CCP, but active understanding and participation in the regime's goals. Education is a prime factor in achieving these ends, and is designed both to replace the former Confucian scale of values, with its loyalty to the family rather than the state and its disdain for manual labour, with a new communist morality, and to produce men and women equipped with the skills required by a society on the road to modernisation and industrialisation. True communist man must therefore be both "red" and "expert", politically conscious and professionally competent.

Since 1949 there has been a steady quantitative improvement in education facilities. In 1949, 80 per cent of the total population were illiterate. Although it is probable that even now, 50 per cent of the older generation are still illiterate, nine out of ten of the younger generation have at least functional literacy. One of the major obstacles to literacy is the ideographic nature of the Chinese language, together with its many differing dialects. The communists have popularised and spread the standard pronunciation, simplified many of the more common characters, and are working towards the latinisation of Chinese script.

The full-time educational structure is divided into three major parts; primary, secondary and higher or university level. Primary education begins at the age of seven, lasts for six years, and is attended by virtually all children in the urban areas, and over 80 per cent of those in the rural areas, although major efforts were made during the Great Leap of 1958-9 to make this as universal in the countryside as in the cities.

Secondary education also lasts for six years, with two stages of middle school, upper and lower, of three years each. About 10 per cent of those completing primary education continue to middle school. In addition to middle school, there are also normal schools for teacher training, and technical schools. Ten per cent of those completing secondary education will go on to full-time higher education at the university level— either universities, polytechnics, medical schools or agricultural and engineering institutes. It is estimated that there are one million such students at present, most of them in engineering and medicine.

In addition to these full-time educational facilities, there is also spare-time education, with classes run after working hours by the trades unions with a wide range from simple literacy to university level classes. Part-time schools are arranged in the agricultural areas during winter-time. Finally, there are part-work, part-study programmes, which were begun in the rural areas in 1958. Students spend half their time in the schools (either secondary or higher levels) and half working.

They therefore benefit educationally, as well as acquiring a "proletarian viewpoint" through experience of manual labour. About one person in four in China is receiving some kind of educational training.

In spite of an announced bias towards the proletariat and peasantry, the CCP found that it was still the children of bourgeois families who were receiving a major share of advanced education. By dint of strenuous efforts, the percentage of children from worker and peasant backgrounds of the total university enrolment was raised from 20 per cent in 1952 to 50–60 per cent in 1964. However, in recent years, concurrently with the stress on "redness" or political reliability, there has been the fear of a rebirth of capitalism, and a belief that the new youth are untrustworthy. This problem, as seen by the Party, is one of "how to ensure the revolution, won by the older generation at the cost of such sacrifices, will be carried on victoriously to the end by generations to come; that the destiny of our country will continue to be held secure in the hands of true proletarian revolutionaries; that our sons and grandsons and their successors will continue to advance, generation after generation, along the Marxist–Leninist, and not the revisionist, path, that is, advance steadily towards the goal of communism, and not to retreat to make room for a capitalist restoration".[5] This problem of the "heirs and successors to the revolution" was a continuing theme of the Cultural Revolution.

University teachers and administrators were caught up in the cultural revolutionary purges of 1966. In June of that year, a joint notice of the Central Committee and the State Council announced a postponement of new enrolment for six months while reforms were worked out in the old system of entrance examinations in order to "root out bourgeois domination" and ensure that more "revolutionary young people from among the workers, peasants and soldiers" would enter the higher educational institutions.[6] By the end of the six-months hiatus, however, school functioning was totally halted by the disruptive activities of the Red Guards. A return to study was authorised in February and March 1967, but met

[5] *Peking Review*, no. 30 (24 July 1964), p. 19.
[6] ibid., no. 26 (24 June 1966), p. 3.

with little response, and continual bloody clashes in the educational sector led to the army being called in to restore order in the summer. Following threats from Chou En-lai in September concerning cancellation of registration and non-recognition of graduation, there was a half-hearted return to classes in October 1967, although damage to classrooms and equipment had still to be repaired; teachers hesitated to return for fear of further humiliation at the hands of their students, and the students themselves were reluctant to relinquish the more exciting life of exchanging "revolutionary experiences" with other groups.

Law and order was still not restored by the end of the year, and discussion of reforms of the enrolment system, administration, teaching methods and curricula continued. Further factional violence was reported during early 1968. With the widespread "exile" of former Red Guards to remote frontier areas, a semblance of order had been restored by 1969, though the educational reforms were still to be put into concrete form. In all probability the forecast is that the compression of courses and lowering of standards required to allow more workers and peasants to enter higher education will result in a general lowering of educational standards.

Intellectuals

The Chinese definition of "intellectual" (literally *chih-shih fen-tzu,* or "knowledgeable element") is much broader than that operative in the West, since it includes all those who have completed a Chinese higher middle school education. Many, if not the majority of these intellectuals are to be found in the ranks of the bureaucracy. In the 1955–8 period the total number of intellectuals was put at between four and five million.

In an industrialising society where the need for skills is high, the intellectuals are in demand. However, in addition to needing their talents, the CCP also distrusted them. Since access to education was limited pre-1949, most intellectuals were of "bourgeois origin", their training based on Western concepts of education, and often received abroad, particularly in the United States. The Party therefore sought on the one hand to make use of the existing intellectuals by making them politically reliable through thought reform, and on the other hand to train a new generation of revolutionary intellectuals from the worker and peasant classes.

The latter policy was not very successful, as the new intellectuals still tended to manifest such bourgeois characteristics as putting personal and professional interests before those of Party and state, so that, increasingly, the Party was filled, at least at its lower levels, with men of lesser ability than the intellectuals, who stood by as passive onlookers. In their attempts ideologically to remould and make use of the intellectuals, to make them both red and expert, the Party's policies fluctuated between periods of harshness and relaxation, with each campaign against the intellectuals being followed by their withdrawal from any work that might be open to political criticism, by refusing to innovate, by becoming passive bystanders, waiting until the Party once again needed their skills, and was forced to relax the pressure.[7]

For the first two years after assuming power in 1949 the CCP attempted to transform the intellectuals into willing instruments of the state by persuasion rather than coercion. Many intellectuals went through the process of thought reform (or "brain-washing") in "revolutionary colleges", where they learned to purge themselves of their evil bourgeois heritage and to be re-born in the communist image. By confessing their "errors" and indulging in self-criticism, the intellectuals, it was hoped, would rid themselves of egotism and professionalism, distrust of the USSR and emulation of America. By eliminating potential opposition, the regime hoped to consolidate its control over the population.

Some relaxation followed in late 1953 and early 1954 as the start of the first Five Year Plan necessitated the active cooperation of all skilled personnel. However, a far more significant episode began in 1956, when following a conference of the CCP Central Committee in January, a period of relaxation was begun which culminated in the famous 100 Flowers movement of 1957.

It was apparent in the closing years of the first Five Year Plan that the economy was running out of steam, and that

[7] See Merle Goldman, "The Unique 'Blooming and Contending' of 1961–1962", *China Quarterly*, no. 37 (January–March, 1969), pp. 54–83.

the experts needed to be called in to rectify the situation. However, over the years, they had become steadily disenchanted with life under communism. Speaking to the January conference therefore, Chou En-lai admitted past errors in the treatment of the intellectuals, estimated that only 45 per cent of them actively supported the CCP, and promised a liberalisation in their treatment, and better conditions of life. This was to be linked to a campaign to bring the more "progressive" elements among them into the CCP.

The slogan "Let a Hundred Flowers Blossom, a Hundred Schools of Thought Contend", which referred back to the period of the Chou dynasty in Chinese history, was proclaimed by Mao in a speech given on 2 May 1956. In a speech of that title delivered later that month by Lu Ting-yi, head of the Central Committee's Propaganda Department, he advocated freedom of criticism, in order to produce a flourishing art of literature, and advances in science.

The intellectuals did not react enthusiastically to the Party's overtures. Party insistence on more freedom of thought and criticism was possibly heightened by Khrushchev's "de-Stalinisation" speech of February 1956, and by the Hungarian uprising in October of that year. On 27 February 1957 Mao Tse-tung delivered his speech "On the Correct Handling of Contradictions among the People", in which he encouraged the 100 Flowers movement. Again the response was not very encouraging to the Party. Finally, in May, following a resolution of the Central Committee of 27 April in which a rectification of the Party was advocated, the dam burst, and non-Party personnel were urged to participate in criticising Party cadres, and curing the Party of its defects. The criticisms that appeared were stronger, and more to the point than the Party had bargained for. Often using the language of Western democracy, intellectuals and students blossomed into activity with wall-posters denouncing the monopoly of power of the CCP, and the arrogant attitudes of Party members. For five weeks a vitriolic campaign continued against all aspects of communist rule. Finally on June 8, the Party, stunned and shaken, cracked the whip and began purging as "rightists" those intellectuals who had had the temerity to voice their dislike of the regime. Clearly the Party could not permit its

ight to a monopoly of power to be challenged, and so the
ragrant flowers became poisonous weeds, and the uprooting
n the form of the anti-rightist campaign continued throughout
957, while freedom of criticism was restricted once again
o academic debate within the framework of the communist
ystem. The intellectuals were sent down to the countryside
n increasing numbers to take part in manual labour, and
vith the euphoria of the Great Leap of 1958, redness more
nd more took precedence over expertise.

However, the failure of the Great Leap, economic decline,
nd the withdrawal of Soviet technicians in the summer of
1960, forced the Party to once more embark on a policy of
attempting to win the cooperation of the intellectuals in order
to rehabilitate the economy from the three bitter years of
1959–61. This led to a partial revival of the 100 Flowers
movement from the spring of 1961 to the summer of 1962.
This time, a strict framework was laid down for liberalisation,
separating academic from political discussion, and prohibiting
any expression of anti-Party sentiments. Such discussion as
there was had to conform to criteria such as being beneficial
to socialist transformation and to the strengthening of the
CCP leadership.[8] And even this brief period of mild relaxation came to an end following the Tenth Plenum of the CC
in September 1962, as the economic indicators began to move
up and the Party regained confidence. From this time on, it
was once again "politics in command".

In 1963 another campaign was launched against the intellectuals, this time by Chou Yang (subsequently purged during the Cultural Revolution), who warned of a possible capitalist restoration in China if Soviet revisionism was allowed
to spread through the intellectuals. From 1965 onwards, many
intellectuals in the cultural, teaching, journalism and propaganda fields were purged, as the Party claimed that "the
bourgeois 'experts', 'scholars', 'authorities' and 'respected mas-
ters' and their like have been routed, and their arrogance
has been completely shattered".[9]

[8] See Dennis J. Doolin, "The Revival of the 100 Flowers Campaign:
1961. *China Quarterly*, no. 8 (October–December, 1961), pp. 34–41.
[9] *The Great Socialist Cultural Revolution in China*, no. 5 (Peking:
Foreign Languages Press, 1966), p. 1.

However, surveying the wreckage in the aftermath of the Cultural Revolution, there were indications that the Party once again was seeing the need for the cooperation of the intellectuals. Lin Piao, speaking to the Ninth Party Congress, was himself an example of the new approach by comparison with the hostile attitudes of past years, when he stated that "the majority, or the vast majority, of the intellectuals trained in the old type of schools and colleges are able, or willing, to integrate themselves with the workers, peasants and soldiers. . . ."[10] Although the Party is in need of experienced administrators to run the state, there is doubt whether this period of "relaxation" will last any longer than its predecessors.

National minorities

The national minorities, or non-Han Chinese, make up only 6 per cent of the entire population of China, but they occupy 50–60 per cent of the total land area of the country. The best land for cultivation is populated by the Hans, with the national minorities living on relatively barren steppes and mountains, and making a living as herdsmen. The areas inhabited by the national minorities are frequently rich in minerals and are often of strategic importance. All together there are more than fifty different minority races, the largest being the Chuang (7.7 million), with the Uighurs, Mongols, Tibetans, Hui (Moslems), and Koreans also having populations in excess of one million. Most of them are economically and socially backward compared with the Hans. The chief characteristics differentiating them from each other and from the Hans (apart from the fact that the national minorities are mainly pastoralists) are language and religion. The Islamic faith claims the largest number of adherents, followed by the Lamaists of Tibet.

Before the communists came to power, they emphasised the right to self-determination for all national minorities. The 1931 Constitution of the Chinese Soviet Republic specified that they had the right to complete separation from China, and the right to form independent states. On their assumption

[10] New China News Agency (27 April 1969).

of control over the mainland, however, the CCP proclaimed the People's Republic of China to be a "unitary, multi-national state", and the 1954 Constitution, while giving the minority areas a certain degree of administrative autonomy, and freedom to use their own language and preserve their customs, declared that these areas were an inseparable part of China.

Special administrative areas have been set up for the national minorities. The largest of these is the Autonomous Region (AR), of which there are five. The first to be established was the Inner Mongolian AR (1947), followed by the Sinkiang–Uighur AR (1955), the Kwangsi–Chuang AR (1958), the Ninghsia–Hui AR (1958) and finally the Tibet AR (1965). There are also a wide variety of smaller autonomous administrative units. Within the CCP, national minorities policy is handled primarily by the United Front Work Department of the Central Committee.

A gradualist approach was followed by the CCP in its policy towards the national minorities for the first few years after 1949. There was no great pressure for reform, and although many cadres were sent into the minority areas (so that the Hans eventually became a majority in areas such as Inner Mongolia), they were ordered not to commit the cardinal sin of "great Han chauvinism" in their attitudes towards the minority peoples.

This gradualist policy began to change in 1956 with the implementation of long-deferred reforms in the minority areas. The widespread anti-rightist campaign of 1957 became one of opposing "local nationalism" among the minority peoples, and there were attempts to substitute Chinese for the local languages. The minority areas also became caught up in the Great Leap Forward and it was stated that they would catch up with the Hans within a few years. However, the Great Leap was even less successful in the minority areas than elsewhere in the country.

In line with overall Party policy in the aftermath of the Great Leap, a more moderate policy was manifested towards the minorities as from the early 1960s, with more concessions to their local peculiarities, and a further deferment of economic and social reforms. In general, the Party has pursued moderate policies towards the national minorities when poor economic and political conditions prevailed, but the long-range aim remains to bring them up to equality with the rest of China.

With the advent of the Cultural Revolution, Party leaders in many minority regions exerted great efforts to avoid having disruption spread to their areas. The Autonomous Regions, with their "backward customs", were clearly prime targets for the reforming zeal of the Red Guards, and many Party authorities were purged or criticised during the Cultural Revolution for their opposition to it. Ulanfu, the leader of the Inner Mongolian AR and a former Politburo member, was not re-elected to either the Politburo or the CC at the Ninth Party Congress. The former leader of the Tibet AR, Chang Kuo-hua, was, however, elected to full CC membership, and the much criticised leader of the Sinkiang–Uighur AR, Wang En-mao, survived, although with a demotion from Politburo to only alternate membership on the new CC.

From the point of view of Peking, the two most strategic national minority areas are those of Sinkiang and Tibet.

Sinkiang

Sinkiang, an area of over 600,000 square miles, and a population of eight million (of which two to three million are Han), has a common border with the Soviet Union, rich mineral deposits, and is of great importance to Peking. The Party has sought to gradually sinicise the area, promote education, and develop its industrial potential. Land reform was carried out on approximately the same timetable as the rest of the country, and there has been considerable investment in petroleum, as well as coal, iron and steel. Sinkiang, in addition to its rich oil reserves, is also the scene of nuclear development, and the nuclear test-site of Lop Nor. Of recent years, considerable tension has developed in the frontier regions bordering the USSR. For the Kazakhs and Uighurs, the Sino-Soviet frontier is an artificial boundary, for their tribes are to be found on both sides of the border. Taking advantage of this fact, the USSR (whose influence in Sinkiang was strong in the 1930s) has made use of local discontent to entice several tens of thousands of minority peoples to seek asylum in the Soviet Union. These incidents were reported to have begun in 1962, with the Chinese claiming thousands of border violations by the Russians since that time.

Tibet

Tibet is the most socially and culturally backward, and physically remote of all the Autonomous Regions. Although of strategic importance, it possesses little of economic value. Nevertheless, it has always been considered by successive Chinese rulers to be a part of China, and was invaded by the PLA in October 1950. Agreement was reached with the Dalai Lama, the ruler of Tibet, for the occupation of the country. Although now under the control of the CCP, the country did not experience any great reforms, and was left virtually undisturbed. However, when collectivisation of agriculture was implemented in neighbouring Szechuan in 1956, it aroused the resistance of the Khambas, a pastoral people, who fled to Tibet and instigated resistance among the Tibetans to Chinese rule. This led to the Tibetan rebellion of 1959, and the fleeing of the Dalai Lama to India. Shortly after the rebellion was suppressed the CCP began to carry out "socialist reforms" in Tibet, and to push ahead with preparations for the area to become a fully-fledged Autonomous Region. The Tibet AR was formally inaugurated in September 1965 under the authority of Chang Kuo-hua (a Han Chinese, and CCP administrative and military leader), although with a Tibetan in nominal control. During the Cultural Revolution, Tibet saw considerable factional fighting between differing Red Guard groups, aggravated by the continued resistance of Tibetans to Chinese rule.

Marriage and the family

In pre-communist China, the family was the basic unit of society, with authority vested in the hands of the eldest male in the household. From the standpoint of its individual members, therefore, the family, not the state, was the primary unit to which they owed loyalty. The women in the family were subordinate to the men, and marriage was far too important an affair to be left to the discretion of the couple themselves. On the contrary, for the traditional Chinese family marriage was not so much an affair of the matured children as an affair of the parents and of the family, with its chief purpose not so much the romantic happiness of the marrying children but fulfilling the sacred duty of producing male heirs for the perpetuation of the ancestors' lineage, the acquiring of a daughter-in-law for the service and comfort of the parents, and the begetting of sons for the security of the parents' old age.[11]

The foundations of this traditional family structure had been somewhat eroded as from the latter half of the nineteenth century with the start of industrialisation and the introduction of Western concepts of personal freedom and individual rights, and this erosion had been accelerated with the general collapse of authority that took place after the fall of the dynasty in 1911, and the decline of the Republic into civil war. During this period the Kuomintang did attempt reforms of the social structure, but by and large Westernisation was confined to the wealthier classes in the urban areas.

A basic aim of the CCP on coming to power was to destroy the archaic, feudal form of the traditional family structure, while retaining the family as a basic social unit. In the new-style family, it was envisaged that women would have equal rights with men, that many of the women's traditional functions would be taken over by the state, thereby releasing them for productive labour, that there would be freedom of marriage, and thus horizons of individual members would be widened so that loyalty would be given, not to the family, but to the collective and to the state. In many respects, therefore, the changes demanded by the communists were those that would be felt by any family structure in an industrialising society.

With the new Marriage Law promulgated in May 1950, the practices of concubinage, child marriage, and payment for brides were all prohibited. A minimum age was set for marriage at twenty for men and eighteen for women, and the marriage ceremony itself became a simple affair of the couple

---

[11] C. K. Yang, *Chinese Communist Society: The Family and the Village* (Cambridge, Mass.: MIT Press, 1965), "The Chinese Family in the Communist Revolution", p. 23.

registering with the local *hsiang* government. Women were given equal rights in the home with men, and divorce was to be granted freely when both husband and wife requested it. Needless to say, with so many unhappy marriages which had been "arranged" by the parents under the old system, the years following the passage of the Marriage Law witnessed a substantial increase in the divorce rate, which reached almost 400,000 in the first six months of 1952 alone. The enforcement of the Marriage Law was a primary responsibility of the All-China Federation of Democratic Women, whose Vice-Chairman was Teng Ying-ch'ao (the wife of Chou En-lai), and which had a membership of seventy-six million in 1953. Their main task was to ensure that the Law was enforced in the more backward rural areas. The Federation also acted to oppose discrimination against women and to liberate women from the home to take part in productive labour as the state increasingly took over the functions of education and care of the elderly. This trend reached a high point with the Great Leap Forward, when the communes provided communal cooking facilities. This met with widespread peasant resistance, and the influence of the communes declined. There is evidence, however, of continuing resistance to change in the traditional ways in the rural areas, for during the Cultural Revolution, there were reports of children being urged to oppose the old concept of filial piety by rebelling against their parents if the parent's words were not in conformity with the "Thought of Mao Tse-tung", as well as reports of continued discrimination against women, and requests from Party officials for couples not to have a lavish old-fashioned wedding, but to economise with a "revolutionary wedding ceremony", after working hours.

Nevertheless, women have joined the labour force in increasing numbers, and have established a great degree of equality with men in both work and the home, as well as strictly legal equality. A general atmosphere of puritanism pervades the country, and young people are urged to defer marriage until age thirty for men and twenty-five for women. Family planning is also encouraged. Many women hold positions of authority in local government, and are elected as delegates to the National People's Congress. Few, however, reach the highest positions of power, although several wives of prominent Party members are members of the Ninth Central Committee, including Chiang Ch'ing (Mrs Mao Tse-tung), Yeh Ch'ün (Mrs Lin Piao), Teng Ying-ch'ao (wife of Chou En-lai), Ts'ai Ch'ang (wife of Li Fu-ch'un) and Ts'ao Yi-ou (married to K'ang Sheng).

6

FOREIGN POLICY

Overview

For a variety of reasons stemming from historical experiences, ideological considerations and economic and political factors, the current leadership of the CCP is one that is highly dissatisfied with the present global configuration of power, and is a leadership that therefore sees China as a major force for changing the *status quo*. At the same time, Chinese foreign policy, like that of any other nation state, is designed to achieve such basic aims as the preservation of territorial security, defence of the state against external attack, unification of the state's territory and the creation of a sphere of influence among neighbouring states.

With respect to all these aims, the power of the United States looms large as a force preventing Peking from attaining many of its foreign-policy objectives. Peking has long perceived that the major hazard to its territory stems from American military bases around its borders in South Korea, Japan, Okinawa, Taiwan, the Philippines, South Vietnam and Thailand, as well as the presence of the US Seventh Fleet in the Western Pacific, and the threat of a possible strategic thermonuclear strike. More recently, however, China has also come to feel threatened from the other global super-power, the Soviet Union.

Therefore, in addition to assigning a high priority to the creation of a credible nuclear deterrent capability of its own, China seeks to eliminate US bases and influence in Southeast Asia and East Asia, believing that a leading role in Asia is China's right, on political, cultural and historical grounds. Specifically, China aims not at the military occupation of the states on her borders, but insists on the viability of the communist regimes in North Korea and North Vietnam, and seeks a zone of friendly buffer states in the rest of the area.

The Chinese leaders would also like to extend their influence in the rest of the underdeveloped areas of the world, and see their country as a suitable model for emulation in the fields of political and economic development.

Further high-priority objectives include territorial unification (particularly with respect to Taiwan), the acknowledgement by all of China's great power status (by being consulted on all major international issues, seating in the United Nations, and a position on the Security Council), and the replacement of the Soviet Union by China as the ideological authority in the communist world.

Both China's distant and recent history are major determinants of her foreign policy. For several millennia, China was politically, culturally, and economically superior to her immediate neighbours. Relations between states were those between superiors and inferiors, and not the European concept of legal equality between countries. More recent events have reinforced China's belief in her historical role to a paramount position in Asia and world affairs, for the life experiences of the present generation of communist leaders, combined with an awareness of the humiliations suffered by China during the past century, have also created in their minds a belief that (over a long period of time) human will and perseverance can achieve victory against overwhelming odds. Just as the CCP sees itself to have achieved such a victory over the KMT, so it sees China as ultimately victorious against both the United States and the Soviet Union.

These historical determinants are further sustained by ideological considerations, for in the prevailing belief-system of Marxism–Leninism–Maoism, the communist leaders see their country as historically destined to be the true standard bearer of revolution, in the forefront of the struggle for the establishment of communism on a global scale.

While China has in many ways adopted a posture of belligerence, chauvinism and xenophobia towards the outside world, day-to-day management of foreign policy has been characterised by caution, low risk-taking, and a real awareness of the actual balance of forces in the world. In particular, in spite of unremitting hostility towards the United States, China has been careful to avoid a major confrontation.

On coming to power in October 1949 the Chinese communists immediately called for diplomatic recognition, which was received over the ensuing seven months, from the whole communist bloc (including Yugoslavia), Scandinavia, Israel, the Netherlands, Switzerland, the United Kingdom, and six Asian countries, Afghanistan, Burma, Ceylon, India, Indonesia and Pakistan. Recognition was soon reciprocated in all cases with the exception of Yugoslavia, which was delayed for five years. The establishment of diplomatic relations was also delayed for years in the case of several of these countries, and were never established with Israel. In addition to appealing for diplomatic recognition, China also claimed membership of the United Nations, and the right to the permanent seat on the UN Security Council.

The early years of Chinese foreign policy were marked by close relations with the USSR, inaugurated after Mao Tse-tung visited Moscow in December 1949 to negotiate aid and trade agreements, resulting in the Sino–Soviet Treaty of Friendship and Alliance in February 1950. Some months before the formal creation of the People's Republic, Mao had announced that China would:

externally, unite in a common struggle with those nations of the world which treat us as equals and unite with the peoples of all countries. That is, ally ourselves with the Soviet Union, with the People's Democracies and with the proletariat and the broad masses of the people in all other countries, and form an international united front.[1]

This policy was described by Mao as "leaning to one side", to the side of socialism, and at the same time he denied the existence of a "third road" in between imperialism and socialism.[2]

Up until 1951, the outlook of the Chinese communist leadership towards the rest of the world was an extremely militant one. They tended to see their revolutionary strategy which had brought them success as a suitable model for the

[1] Mao Tse-tung, "On the People's Democratic Dictatorship", *Selected Works*, vol. IV, p. 415.
[2] ibid.

underdeveloped world. Their policy was consequently one of hostility to neutralist Asian and African states who were trying to pursue a "third road" between capitalism and communism, combined with support for armed uprisings in Burma, Malaya, Indo-China and the Philippines. However, with the exception of material aid given to the Vietminh in Indo-China, such support was confined to the level of propaganda backing.

Although the attack by North Korea on its southern neighbour in June 1950 seems to have been engineered by Stalin without consulting his Chinese allies, the Korean War nevertheless had important implications for the PRC. The first effect of the war was that President Truman changed US policy towards China, declared that an invasion of Taiwan by mainland forces would threaten US security in the Far East, and promptly interposed the Seventh Fleet between the island and the mainland, in the vicinity of which it has remained ever since, preventing the "liberation" of Taiwan by the communists. In seeking a quick victory over South Korea, Stalin miscalculated the US reaction; subsequently, the influx of troops under United Nations command expelled the communists from South Korea, penetrated North Korea, and approached the Manchurian border of China. Then the Chinese felt their security to be in danger, and intervened in the war in October 1950 with a massive commitment of "volunteers". The intervention, which cost the Chinese dearly in men and equipment, also hindered their prospects of entering the UN since they were dubbed the aggressor in the war. However, the PRC did help secure the continued existence of a friendly communist buffer state, and established China's right to have a voice in the settlement of Asian problems by participating in the peace negotiations which began in July 1951. Finally, although the UN forces had been pushed back to the 38th parallel, China's conflict with modern Western firepower and air superiority convinced the bulk of the Chinese leadership that further direct clashes with the United States had best be avoided for the foreseeable future.

From 1951 onwards Chinese foreign policy increasingly veered away from the dogmatic insistence on armed struggle typical of the earlier period, and de-emphasised hostility towards the new states of Asia and Africa. A number of factors caused the shift in line: the losses sustained in Korea; the lack of success of armed struggle abroad (with the exception of Indo-China); the growth of US-sponsored collective security agreements like the Southeast Asia Treaty Organisation (SEATO); and the increasing need to concentrate on domestic issues such as the start of the first Five Year Plan in 1953.

In 1953 a truce agreement was finally signed in Korea, and the following year the Geneva Conference over Vietnam, in which the PRC played a leading role, reached agreement over the division of Vietnam pending the holding of a general election. In 1954 Foreign Minister Chou En-lai and India's Prime Minister Nehru issued a joint declaration on peaceful coexistence between states which included the principles of non-aggression, non-interference in each other's internal affairs, and respect for each other's territory. At the same time, India acknowledged the validity of the Chinese claim to Tibet, which had been invaded and occupied by China in October 1950.

The neutralist countries of the underdeveloped world were further impressed by the conciliatory policies of the PRC when Chou En-lai reiterated the principles of peaceful coexistence at the Conference of Asian and African States held at Bandung, Indonesia, in April 1955. At the Conference, Chou offered to negotiate with the United States over the question of Taiwan, and talks between the two countries began in Geneva in August 1955.

At the Twentieth Congress of the CPSU held in Moscow in 1956, Khrushchev launched his attack on Stalin, which was a major factor in the Hungarian and Polish uprisings that occurred later that year. These uprisings caused fears of similar events in China which, together with the unsuccessful attempts at liberalisation of the 100 Flowers campaign, led to a policy of domestic repression, which was mirrored in a more rigid line abroad. This return to a more militant and antagonistic foreign policy towards all states not considered to be equally hostile towards the Western powers was given added impetus with the announcement by the Soviet Union in 1957 of the testing of an inter-continental ballistic missile and the launching of the world's first space satellite, in August and October respectively. The Chinese saw these technological successes as a manifestation of Soviet superiority over the United States. Maintaining that "the East wind prevails over the West wind", the Chinese leaders urged the USSR to take advantage of their achievements by pursuing a vigorous anti-Western policy. The Soviet leaders' lack of agreement with this view, combined with their ideologically derived hostility towards China's Great Leap Forward of 1958 and opposition to the extravagant claims made for the people's communes, plus their obvious lack of support for the Chinese position during the PRC's clash with the Nationalists over the offshore Islands of Quemoy and Matsu in the summer of that year, were major factors in exacerbating the dispute between the two communist powers.

The Tibetan rebellion of 1959, and the flight of the Dalai Lama to sanctuary in India brought Chinese and Indian troops into conflict in the disputed frontier regions, although full-scale war did not break out until 1962. The brief period of hostilities in that year resulted in certain small, but strategic gains for China, and a humiliating defeat for India, the chief counter-weight to the PRC in Asia. Pre-occupied with internal problems caused by economic failure, China was less active on the global scene during the early 1960s, although attempts were made by the PRC, particularly in the first half of the decade, to increase its influence in the Afro-Asian world, and to create a bloc of "third world" countries hostile to both the West and the Soviet Union.

In 1965, Lin Piao, now installed as the successor to Mao Tse-tung, re-emphasised the Maoist doctrine for world revolution in his "Long Live the Victory of People's War", which divided the world into the underdeveloped "countryside", destined to encircle and defeat the "cities of the world", namely the United States and Western Europe. Revolution in the "world countryside" was envisioned as being carried out mainly by indigenous groups relying on their own resources, and emulating the Chinese model.

With the chaos of the Cultural Revolution, Chinese foreign policy became moribund, with few positive initiatives emanating from Peking. The process of foreign-policy making was disrupted in mid-1967 when rampaging Red Guards occupied

and sacked the Foreign Ministry in Peking, causing a temporary cessation of work by Ministry personnel. In the same year,
all ambassadors were recalled (with the exception of the ambassador to the United Arab Republic), and their return only
began following the Ninth Party Congress in 1969. Meanwhile, Chinese foreign policy continued to run along the
familiar lines of hostility towards both the United States and
the Soviet Union. The only change was the apparent replacement of America by Russia as China's number one
enemy, a change manifested in the speech made by Lin Piao
to the Ninth Party Congress in April 1969, and due no doubt
to the continuing armed clashes between the two countries
along their common border in Manchuria and Sinkiang.

Sino–Soviet breach

Even before 1956, which is the date usually taken as the
starting point for the rift between the two powers, it was clear
that there were historical disagreements of long standing between the two parties; the ineptitude of Stalin's policies that
resulted in the massacre of the CCP in 1927 (the Chinese
commented ruefully in 1963 "long ago [we] had first-hand
experience of some of his mistakes"); Stalin's support for
Chiang Kai-shek after the Second World War; and his dismantling of Manchurian industry are only examples. However,
the Chinese waited until 1956 and the Twentieth Congress
of the CPSU, three years after the death of Stalin, and when
their position at home was well consolidated, to make their
challenge on the fundamental question of authority within
the communist bloc.

At the Twentieth Party Congress in Moscow, Khrushchev
made his famous de-Stalinisation speech debunking the
former dictator, and revising traditional Marxism–Leninism
on a number of fundamental points. Even without considera-
tion of the revisions, the Chinese felt insulted because they
had neither been consulted nor informed in advance of the
speech, and Mao was probably doubly furious, since he considered himself to be the greatest living communist theorist.
The Chinese had a higher regard for Stalin than the Russians:
while admitting that "he was sometimes divorced from reality
and from the masses", and that he made "certain mistakes",

they nevertheless concluded that "Stalin's merits and mistakes are matters of historical, objective reality. A comparison of the two shows that his merits outweighed his faults".[3]

The major revisions of theory were on three counts: Soviet foreign policy of "peaceful coexistence" with the West; the assertion that war was no longer "fatalistically inevitable"; and the belief that in some advanced industrial capitalist societies the transition to a socialist system could be accomplished peacefully, by parliamentary methods. With respect to their foreign policy, the Russians believed that the Soviet Union and the socialist camp as a whole were now strong enough to deter the "imperialists" from initiating a major war, so that the superiority of the socialist system would be demonstrated by peaceful competition in economic and technical progress. This, and the Soviet assertion of the possibility of a peaceful transition to socialism in capitalist countries, clearly reflected the impact of nuclear weapons on Soviet policy, as well as the USSR's orientation towards the industrial sector of the world as the focus for the spread of communism. Clearly, the concept of peaceful coexistence implied a détente between Russia and America, and consequent lack of Soviet support for Chinese foreign policy goals in Asia, where the United States was China's chief enemy. The Chinese, on the other hand, saw the underdeveloped world as being in the front line of the battle against imperialism, and wanted the Soviet Union to use its political and economic strength in these areas to support the struggle against the West. At the same time, while agreeing that war was no longer "fatalistically inevitable", the Chinese disagreed that anything but a violent revolution would dislodge capitalism in Europe or the United States, and urged that armed struggle be the main weapon used in the underdeveloped countries. The Chinese, therefore, were more confident than the Russians that wars of "national liberation" in these areas would not escalate into a nuclear exchange.[4]

A major problem for Khrushchev during this exchange was that since he had debunked Stalin, he therefore prevented

[3] "On the Question of Stalin", *Peking Review*, no. 38 (20 September 1963), pp. 9–10.
[4] For more details of Chinese nuclear weapons policy, see Chapter 4.

himself from inheriting the mantle of Stalin's prestige and authority within the communist bloc, which had been a major factor in maintaining the position of the USSR in determining the ideological line for the bloc as a whole. The Chinese were eventually to set themselves up as the only valid interpreters of true Leninist orthodoxy. However, in the history of the Sino–Soviet rift, it is clear that ideology, although a major determinant in the attitudes of both sides, and a medium for debate, has played a minor role compared to such factors as great power status, national interest and historical considerations.

The views of the Chinese concerning the need for a concerted offensive against the West were bolstered by Soviet advances in rocketry during 1957, and Mao Tse-tung, at a meeting of the world's ruling communist parties held in Moscow following the celebrations for the Fortieth anniversary of the Bolshevik Revolution, took the opportunity to reiterate his belief that the "East wind is prevailing over the West wind" and press for a more forceful foreign policy. In spite of their technical advances, the Russians were no more willing than before to concede to his arguments, and the meeting produced only an ambiguously worded document in the form of the 1957 Moscow Declaration, which condemned both "revisionism" and "sectarianism and dogmatism".

Moscow's reluctance to support Peking's foreign policy objectives was amply demonstrated during the "offshore island" crisis of August 1958, when the Chinese communists shelled the Nationalist-held islands of Quemoy and Matsu. A firm statement of the commitment from Khrushchev was obtained only after the crisis had died down, indicating a complete lack of coordination in Sino–Soviet foreign policy. The rift between the two sides was widened in 1958 by China's Great Leap Forward, during which claims were made for the people's communes to the effect that they contained the "buds of communism", so that China would achieve communism before its economically more advanced rival, the Soviet Union. The Chinese also said that the Great Leap Forward was a suitable model for the underdeveloped world, for which countries Russian revolutionary experience was irrelevant.

After studiously remaining neutral in the Sino–Indian

border dispute of 1959, Khrushchev went to the United States to confer with President Eisenhower at Camp David, following which he arrived in Peking, only to suggest to the Chinese that they adopt the *de facto* recognition of "two Chinas" as a solution to the Taiwan problem, and to urge them not to "test by force the stability of the capitalist system". In the same year, the Soviet Union reneged on its promise to supply China with a sample atom bomb.

From this time on, the gap between the two powers widened at an accelerating rate. In the spring of 1960 the Chinese launched a series of open polemics attacking the length and breadth of Soviet policies. In June of that year the dispute took on an "organisational form" as the Chinese criticised Soviet policies at a meeting of an international communist front organisation, the World Federation of Trades Unions, held in Peking, and openly tried to win the allegiance of other communist parties from the Russians. That summer the Russians withdrew all their remaining experts from China.

The meeting of the world's eighty-one communist parties in Moscow that November was the first major attempt to reconcile differences. However, only a stalemate compromise was reached, with most parties supporting the Soviet Union, and just Albania fully supporting Peking. Less than a year later, at the twenty-second Congress of the CPSU (October 1961), Khrushchev delivered a lengthy attack on Albania (and implicitly on China) and broke off diplomatic relations with Albania shortly afterwards.

The rift deepened in 1962 with the Sino–Indian border war, in which the Soviet Union remained neutral, and then supplied fighter aircraft to India; and with the Cuban missile crisis of that year, as a result of which the Chinese accused the Russians both of "adventurism" (for placing missiles on Cuba in the first place), and "capitulationism" (for removing them under American pressure). The question of the Sino–Soviet border also became a major flash-point in 1962, for the Chinese later (1963) announced that in April–May the Russians had coerced into the Soviet Union more than 60,-000 Chinese living in Sinkiang, and had refused to let them return home. In raising the question of the Sino–Soviet borders in public for the first time, the Chinese also referred to the "unequal treaties" imposed on China by Tsarist Russia in the nineteenth century.

From 1963, as a result of the events in India and Cuba, a switch in Chinese strategy became apparent—from one of attempting to achieve hegemony within the communist bloc to one of setting Peking up as the true source of authority and winning over communist parties to their banner, or splitting parties into two factions. To some extent this process was facilitated by Moscow, who had been forced to relinquish a degree of central control in order to retain the support of other parties. As might have been expected, the initial division of parties was mainly geographical, with the Asian parties (except India) flocking to the Maoist standard, and most of the rest (except Albania) adhering to Moscow. This was to change later, as the intensification of the Vietnam War in 1965 forced Hanoi into greater dependence on Soviet aid, and therefore looser ties to Peking, and with the assertion of greater independence on the part of the Japanese and North Korean parties. The Chinese also began to recognise pro-Chinese factions within other parties as the only legitimate organs.

For the period of the Cultural Revolution, Chinese foreign policy fell into abeyance, although continuing under its own momentum of sustained hostility towards the Soviet Union. But in 1969 the dispute flared up to a hitherto unprecedented degree, with armed clashes erupting in March over an island in the Ussuri River demarcating the Sino–Soviet boundary. Similar clashes were reported from the border in Sinkiang in June. The Ussuri River incidents raised once again the question of the unequal treaties of the nineteenth century, for the land on the other side of the river had been Chinese territory before the treaties. Lin Piao, speaking to the Ninth Party Congress, claimed that in 1964 China had started to negotiate over boundaries with the Soviet Union and that China had agreed to take the unequal treaties as the basis for a settlement. However, in March 1969 the Chinese ominously stated that if the Russians refused to recognise the treaties as unequal, and "if the Soviet side should . . . inexorably refuse to mend its ways, the Chinese side will have to reconsider its position as regards the Sino–Soviet boundary question as a whole".[5] In addition, the Chinese alleged that the Russians had provoked no fewer than 4,189 border incidents since 1964.

The Chinese began to refer to the Russians as "social-imperialists", meaning socialists who acted just like the imperialist powers. On their part, the Russians retorted that Mao Tse-tung had never really understood Marxism–Leninism, the crucial role of the proletariat, and the significance of the communist party. With the Cultural Revolution, Moscow claimed that the CCP had been taken over by a "Maoist group", which had then started the Cultural Revolution, thus liquidating the true CCP, and establishing a "military bureaucratic dictatorship" with great power expansionist ambitions.

In 1969 Soviet leaders brought to fruition an idea of Khrushchev's to hold a further world communist conference. After many delays, the conference finally convened in Moscow in June, for an unparalleled display of disunity. Of the world's eighty-eight parties, seventy-five attended, with five of the fourteen ruling parties absent (including China). Although many delegates, led by the Soviet Union, ritually denounced China, the conference did not result in any excommunication of the Chinese from the communist faith. On the contrary, the degree of polycentrism within the bloc was reflected in the final statement, which did not mention China, but which several parties refused to sign. At least for the foreseeable future, it would seem that the Chinese and the Russians will continue to go their own separate ways.

Peking's revolutionary strategy

In spite of its seemingly bellicose approach to world affairs, Peking is well aware of its own weakness, particularly with reference to American military and political strength, and so adopts a cautious approach, taking care to avoid any direct confrontation with its major enemy. Peking's view of the world is a combination of Chinese ethnocentrism and chauvinism, Maoist ideology, and the revolutionary experiences of the Chinese leaders. The statement made by Lin Piao in September 1965, entitled "Long Live the Victory of People's

[5] Statement of the Chinese Foreign Ministry, 10 March 1969.

War", was a most explicit comment made on Chinese global perceptions, although it only re-stated what had been implicit for many years in both official policy statements and in the writings of Mao Tse-tung. The Chinese claimed that their revolutionary model of a disciplined communist party leading a broad united front, engaged in a protracted armed struggle waged from rural base areas, which had been tried and tested against the KMT, was a suitable model to be used by communist parties in the underdeveloped world. The Chinese saw these armed struggles, or "people's wars", as sweeping over Asia, Africa and Latin America, termed the "world countryside", and so eventually encircling the "cities of the world", namely Western Europe and the United States, just as the CCP had encircled and defeated the KMT, fighting against initially overwhelming odds. With the tide of revolution surging across the "world countryside", the "imperialist forces" would be scattered and weakened, so that ultimately the weak would triumph over the powerful, men would be victorious over weapons, and the West would be revealed as only a "paper tiger", to be taken account of in day-to-day tactics, but to be despised in the long run.

Lin's statement, therefore, was designed to provide guidance for other parties, particularly the Vietnamese, as to how they should handle their strategic tasks, and it stated clearly that these tasks should be accomplished by self-reliance, with no direct military intervention on the part of China, but only limited help.

In Peking's view, therefore, "people's wars" would spring up in many widely scattered places, forcing the United States into wars of attrition, where their forces would be dispersed, and "when the US aggressors are hard pressed in one place, they have no alternative but to loosen their grip on others".[6] By this method, of course, China avoids any direct confrontation with the United States, and yet achieves a maximum of effect with a minimum of expense to itself.

However, this strategy has yet to prove itself as successful, with the exception of the cases of China and possibly Vietnam. Clearly regarded as a test case of "people's war", cer-

[6] Lin Piao, "Long Live the Victory of People's War", *Peking Review*, no. 36 (3 September 1965), p. 26.

tain special conditions apply in Vietnam—such as the capture of an indigenous nationalist movement by local communists, and a common border (for refuge and supply purposes) with China—that are generally absent elsewhere in the world. In fact, the strategy of revolution in the world countryside has proved disadvantageous for Peking in areas such as Africa, where nationalist leaders of newly independent states have no intention of standing by to be swept aside by a communist-led revolution.

Southeast Asia

China tends to regard the Southeast Asian region as an area belonging to its own sphere of influence, one over which it has the right to assert hegemony. Most states in the area, living in the shadow of their giant neighbour to the north, feel that over a period of time the power and influence of Peking will make itself increasingly felt. Certainly geographical proximity makes Southeast Asia the area where Chinese influence can most easily be brought to bear. The main objective, of course, is to remove American political authority and military bases. Ultimately, the Chinese would like to see communist states in the area, but the short-run tactical ambition is to produce neutral governments, friendly to Peking.

Following the French collapse against the communist Vietminh in 1954, the Geneva Conference was convened to decide the future of Vietnam. China's prestige was enhanced by her participation, and it was agreed by the conference that Vietnam should be temporarily partitioned at the 17th Parallel into two regimes, north (communist) and south (non-communist), pending free elections to unify the whole country. It was generally anticipated that the communists under Ho Chi Minh would win the elections. However, the South Vietnamese government, set up under Ngo Dinh Diem and assisted by the United States (which had not signed the Geneva Agreement), refused to permit the elections at the time scheduled. In 1954 the Southeast Asia Treaty Organisation was inaugurated under American auspices, as a collective security pact to guard against any further extension of the influence of either China or the Democratic Republic of Vietnam (North Vietnam) in the area. From 1957 onwards, North Vietnam stepped up its subversion and infiltration of the south, and by capitalising on the political failures of the South Vietnamese government, the point was reached in 1965 where United States forces had to intervene in strength in order to prevent the forcible unification of the country under the control of Hanoi. Although North Vietnam and China share an identity of interest in the Vietnam conflict, their priorities are slightly different, with Hanoi giving first priority to unification, and Peking stressing the need to wear down American strength, and prove the validity of their thesis on "people's war". Both China and the USSR supplied economic and military aid to the North, but China has made it clear that she will not intervene as in Korea unless the existence of North Vietnam should be threatened.

Vietnam's two adjoining states are Cambodia and Laos. Cambodia fears both the Thais and the Vietnamese, her traditional enemies. Since the Americans are allied with Thailand and South Vietnam, and China with North Vietnam, Cambodia has maintained an ambivalent policy, usually friendly towards China,[7] from which it receives economic aid. Laos shares a common border with China, and the latter's main interest is in eliminating American influence and the establishing of a friendly buffer state. Burma signed a boundary agreement with China which was ratified in 1961. In spite of maintaining overtly good relations with the Burmese government, and granting economic aid, China has continued to aid communist insurgents in the north. Ties between the two governments were weakened during the Cultural Revolution, when Peking made use of the Chinese community in Burma for propaganda purposes.

China considers Thailand to be a danger to her security, for Thailand, the only member of SEATO in continental Southeast Asia, supports a large American military presence, which is used in part to prosecute the Vietnam War. The Thais have no common border with China, but the fact that the two countries are separated at one point by only 100 miles of Burmese–Laotian territory has meant that China

[7] Until the overthrow of Prince Sihanouk in March 1970.

can continue to supply aid and equipment to communist guerrillas operating in Northern Thailand.

Of all the states in the area (with the exception of North Vietnam), it is Indonesia with whom China has had the closest relations in the past. Although there were problems in 1959–60 concerning the activities and status of the two and a half million Chinese living in Indonesia, a solution was reached concerning these questions and a Treaty of Friendship signed between the two countries in 1961. Relations were cemented with economic aid from China, Chinese support for Indonesia's "confrontation" with Malaysia, and Indonesian backing of the Chinese call for a second Afro–Asian Conference. Following the election of Malaysia to the United Nations Security Council, China signified her approval when President Sukarno withdrew Indonesia from the UN in 1965. Indonesia then became the centre of China's plan to create an organisation of "newly emergent forces" to act as an anti-UN bloc. However, the situation changed rapidly in September 1965 with the failure of an attempted coup in Indonesia, supported by the Indonesian Communist Party. As a result, Sukarno was deposed, the Indonesian Communist Party (which had been the best organised in the region) virtually eliminated, and its leader, D. N. Aidit, killed. Indonesia soon rejoined the UN and became extremely hostile towards China.

China also has an interest in Southeast Asia because of the presence of an estimated fifteen million "overseas Chinese" in the area, mostly in Thailand, Malaysia–Singapore, Indonesia and Vietnam. Although probably only a minority are devout supporters of Peking's policies, most feel a sense of pride in the achievements of their mother country, and many help China economically with foreign currency remittances to relatives who stayed behind.

Up to this time, Peking's strategy in the Southeast Asian area has met with little success. The policy of armed revolution has had few takers elsewhere in Southeast Asia besides Vietnam, and the areas' non-communist (and even communist governments) have been unwilling to join in an international front, led by Peking in opposition to both the US and the USSR, particularly as Peking cannot match the economic aid of either Moscow or Washington. Relations generally deteriorated during the Cultural Revolution and the attempts to export Maoism abroad, but more moderate policies were faring better in 1969.

South and east Asia

Following 1951, when China somewhat modified her militant policy towards the neutral nations, amicable relations were gradually developed with India. China hoped to draw India into a united front to oppose "imperialism", and the Indians on their part, having one hostile neighbour in Pakistan, decided that it was good policy to be friends with Peking. A trade agreement was signed with India in 1951, and agreement over the Chinese occupation of Tibet was reached in 1954. However, from 1956 onwards, it became clear that Chinese and Indian foreign policies were divergent. The Indians were very dependent on American aid, and could not therefore afford to adopt a militant anti-imperialist policy. Furthermore, the Indians believed that their role as a force for peace in the world was best played by being on good terms with both the USA and the USSR, while Peking's relations with the USSR were deteriorating, and those with the United States could hardly have been worse. Sino–Indian relations continued to worsen as the Indians discovered in 1958 that the Chinese had built a strategic road across Indian territory in the desolate Aksai Chin plateau in the Ladakh region of Northwest India, linking Sinkiang province with Tibet. In 1959 a major border clash occurred, aggravated by the Tibetan rebellion and the acceptance by India of numerous refugees from Tibet, including the Dalai Lama. China then advanced claims to substantial areas of Indian territory both in the Ladakh region and in the North East Frontier Area (NEFA), which again bordered on Tibet, the Chinese claiming that the boundary between Tibet and NEFA, demarcated by the McMahon Line of 1913 had been forced on China by "British aggression".

While entering into diplomatic negotiations over the Sino–Indian border, the Indians began to strengthen their positions in Ladakh and NEFA by building roads and border posts, and by acclimatising troops to fight in the extremely high altitudes encountered in the area. But in October 1962 the Chinese launched a devastating surprise attack in Ladakh and NEFA, demolished Indian resistance, and occupied the areas claimed in 1959, following which they declared a unilateral cease-fire in November, and withdrew their forces from the front.

The motives for the Chinese attack were to conduct a pre-emptive strike before the Indians could entrench themselves in the area, and by so doing win a decisive military and political victory over India—humbling the country that many regarded as an alternative development model for Asian states —and make secure the military highway across the Aksai Chin plateau. Once these limited, but vital objectives were attained, the Chinese ceased fire and withdrew, no doubt aware of logistical difficulties that would be caused by the approaching winter, and also because of the ostentatiously neutral attitude maintained by the Soviet Union during the war.

Ceylon attempted to act as a mediator between the combatants at the Colombo Conference later that year, while both sides continued to strengthen their positions along the actual line of demarcation. The proposals advanced by the Conference were more favourable to the Indian point of view, and were accepted by India, but rejected by China.

One result of the mounting Sino–Indian hostility was an improvement of the association between China and Pakistan. Although the Chinese had initially criticised Pakistan for its membership of SEATO, both sides found it beneficial to improve relations after China's border clashes with India. China wanted to isolate India, and concluded an agreement demarcating the Sino–Pakistan border in 1963. Pakistan felt that she had achieved some protection against Indian attack, and got Peking's support over her long-standing dispute with India concerning Kashmir. The Soviet Union, on the other hand, backed the Indian position in the 1950s, although adopting a neutral posture in the 1960s. Close ties between China and Pakistan have been continued in spite of the Cultural Revolution in China and political changes in Pakistan.

In continuance of the policy of isolating India, China has

cultivated Nepal, signing a boundary agreement in 1969.[8] China is attempting to replace Indian influence in Nepal by Chinese influence, and a further link is being forged by the construction of a road between Katmandu and Tibet.

The presence of US military bases in South Korea, Japan, Okinawa, Taiwan, and the Philippines is viewed by China as a grave threat to its security. Ideally, China would like to see the re-incorporation of Taiwan under the Peking government, the unification of Korea under communist rule, and the neutralisation of Japan and the Philippines, with the consequent removal of much of the US military strength in the area. For China, remembering distant and not so distant history, the fear of a revival of Japanese militarism plays the same role as the fear of a resurgence of German militarism plays in the minds of the Soviet leaders. Japan is also regarded as an economic rival, although the economic relationship also has its beneficial aspects, since Japan is a source of credit, and a supplier of industrial equipment. Accordingly, as official diplomatic relations have yet to be established, the Chinese use the lure of increased trade, plus the influence of leftist, anti-American groups within Japan, to bring pressure on the Japanese government to sever its links with the United States.

The British Crown Colony of Hong Kong, with a total population of about 4 million (the vast majority of which is Chinese) is situated on the Pearl River estuary, opposite the Portuguese territory of Macao on the South China coast. The total land area of Hong Kong is only 400 square miles. The island of Hong Kong itself was ceded to Britain in 1843, as was Kowloon, a small section of the mainland, in 1861. The bulk of the Colony, however, is made up of the so-called New Territories, leased to Britain in 1898. While Peking allows Hong Kong to continue to function at present, mainly because of its value to them as a trading centre and source of hard currency foreign exchange, the Colony is, in a very real sense, living on borrowed time, for the lease on the New Territories expires in 1997. It is highly unlikely that this lease will be renewed, and the Colony cannot exist without the New Territories.

[8] A boundary agreement was also signed with Afghanistan in 1963.

Africa and Latin America

Contact was first established with the states of the Middle East and North Africa at the time of the Asian and Pacific Peace Conference in Peking (1952) and the Bandung Conference of 1955. In 1956, Egypt became the first Middle Eastern country to recognise China. With hostility towards Israel a major factor in Arab foreign policy, China offers her support to the Arab cause, and backs the movement to "liberate Palestine". Peking's ulterior motive in doing so is to erode Western authority in the area, and disrupt the flow of oil to Europe and the United States, while possibly opening up an alternative source of supply for herself.

Peking supported the Algerian National Liberation Front from 1958, supplied them with arms, and recognised the provisional government set up by the Front. Following the establishment of a government under Ben Bella, Algeria became a centre of Chinese influence in North Africa.

In late 1963–early 1964, Premier Chou En-lai made a tour of ten African countries: Algeria, Morocco, Tunisia and the United Arab Republic in North Africa; and Ethiopia, Ghana, Guinea, Mali, Somalia and the Sudan. Chou's visit had a number of objectives: to reduce the influence of Great Britain, the US and the USSR; to improve the relations of African states with China; to reduce support for India over the Sino–Indian War of 1962; and to gain access for China to African markets and resources. Chinese propaganda was marked by racial overtones stressing the need for the solidarity of non-whites against the West and the Russians.

A further major objective was to gather support for the convening of a second Afro–Asian Conference, scheduled to be held in Algeria in 1965. Peking saw the occasion for a "second Bandung" as an opportunity to assert Chinese leadership over a united bloc of African and Asian nations opposed to both American and Soviet "imperialism". However, few African states were willing to go along with Peking. Although Chou En-lai made a second visit to Africa in mid-1965, a coup against Algerian leader Ben Bella led initially to a postponement of the Conference, and then, when it became clear that the Chinese had been unsuccessful in excluding the Soviet Union (on the grounds that the USSR was a European rather than an Asian Power), the Conference was called off, forcing a major diplomatic defeat on the Chinese.

Since that time, relations with most of Africa have continued to deteriorate. Although many African leaders are impressed with the achievements of China, the communists are also competing with Taiwan for influence in the area. In addition, largely because of the ineptitude of its foreign policy, Chinese diplomats have been requested to leave by many African states and over the years there has been a steady growth in the number of African governments opposing the entry of the PRC into the United Nations, ranging from nine in 1965 to twenty in 1968.

Latin America is somewhat on the periphery of Chinese interests, and the record shows only that Peking has given propaganda support to guerrilla movements operating in the area, while expending most of its efforts in factional strife among Latin American communist parties, attempting to get them to oppose the Soviet policy of peaceful transition to socialism. Since Soviet aid is a necessity to Cuba, the Castro government is unwilling to join Peking in an anti-Soviet front, and relations remain cool between the two countries.

The United States, Taiwan and the United Nations

In the period immediately following the communist take-over of the mainland, the United States government was by no means totally hostile towards the idea of recognising the new government of the People's Republic of China. At the same time, with reference to the island of Taiwan (Formosa), to which most of the remaining nationalist forces had fled for refuge, the United States took the view that the island fell outside the American "defence perimeter", and that the eventual fate of the island, and the nationalists on it, was part of the civil war between two warring Chinese factions, with which the United States was no longer concerned.

However, changing events, notably the Korean War, the harsh treatment by the communists of American people and property on the mainland, and the signing of a treaty between the PRC and the Soviet Union, plus domestic reaction to these events, moved the United States into a position of non-recognition of the PRC, plus a policy of diplomatic isolation of its government and the military containment of Chinese communism.

Taiwan therefore became part of the US defence perimeter in the Western Pacific, and the US Seventh Fleet was interposed in the Taiwan Straits between the island and the mainland, thereby effectively preventing a communist invasion directed against the KMT, and also preventing any attempt on the part of Chiang Kai-shek's forces to retake the mainland.

In 1954 a defence treaty was signed between the United States and the Republic of China (Taiwan) providing for US defence of the island. Thus, the security of Taiwan, and the coastal islands of Quemoy and Matsu, are protected by the United States, but the return of the nationalists to the mainland is only a most remote possibility. It should also be noted that the majority of the inhabitants of Taiwan, who have never been on the mainland, would not wish to be reunited with it under any government. American protection, however, has not prevented periodic crises over the offshore islands, with the communists launching heavy bombardments against them in 1954 and again in 1958. As a result of the 1954 crisis, the nationalists were forced to evacuate and abandon to the communists a third group of islands, the Tachens, in early 1955.

The communist position with respect to the establishment of diplomatic relations between themselves and the US is that China (including its outlying province of Taiwan) is one country, that the Republic of China is an illegal "government", backed by the United States which has forcibly intervened in an internal Chinese affair, and that recognition must be accompanied by a settlement of the Taiwan issue—namely, its reincorporation into the mainland under communist auspices. The view that China is one country is probably the only point that the nationalists and the communists have in common, for they both agree that Taiwan is an integral part of China. The disagreement, of course, stems from differing views as to which government constitutes the legitimate ruler of the entire entity. Both governments therefore reject any kind of "two Chinas" solution to the Taiwan problem, by which the territory currently under the *de facto* control of the communists would be recognised as being under their *de jure* control, and Taiwan recognised as a legally independent state with no claim to the mainland. Nevertheless, this would appear to be the direction in which American policy is heading.

For the time being, however, the PRC will not reciprocate any of the US declarations on reducing restrictions on travel to, or trading with, the PRC (part of the overall strategy of "containment without isolation"), stating that these issues and the question of recognition can only be settled contingent on a solution to the Taiwan question, and the withdrawal of US troops from the island and the Taiwan Straits. Indeed it is unlikely that the PRC would deign to recognise the US, even if the US unilaterally recognised the PRC and its claim to the mainland. Nor can it be assumed that recognition of the PRC by the United States would affect the foreign policy of the PRC. Nevertheless, this mutual state of non-recognition has not meant that the United States has had less communication with the PRC than other governments, such as the United Kingdom, which do have diplomatic representatives in each other's capitals. The main channel for these Sino–American communications and negotiations are the meetings which were carried on at ambassadorial level in Geneva from 1955–8, and were subsequently resumed in Warsaw.

Many countries do, or would like to, recognise the PRC diplomatically, but are unwilling to surrender Taiwan to the communists, partially no doubt because of American pressure, but also because few of the Taiwanese would wish it, and the island is a viable political entity in its own right, with a thriving economy and experiencing political development quite separate from the PRC.

The possibility must always be envisaged that the leaders of the PRC and Taiwan will reach some private solution to the problem between themselves. The CCP has never closed the door to the possibility of this event, saying that anyone in Taiwan would be welcomed back to the "embrace of the motherland" if only they would "break away from US imperialist control and be loyal to the motherland".[9] This is most

[9] *Vice-Premier Chen Yi Answers Questions Put by Correspondents* (Peking: Foreign Languages Press, 1966), p. 17.

unlikely to occur, however, while both Mao Tse-tung and Chiang Kai-shek are still alive.

The problem of Taiwan is also intimately bound up with the question of Chinese representation in the United Nations. The question is one of representation, and not admittance, because China was a founder member of the UN, and was given one of the five permanent seats on the UN Security Council. The Chinese seat in the UN and on the Security Council is currently occupied by the Republic of China.

Only one month after the communist victory on the mainland, Chou En-lai claimed that the PRC should be seated in the UN, and the nationalists ejected, on the grounds that the nationalists no longer represented the Chinese people. The PRC no doubt would have been seated, had it not been for the hardening of the US attitude, and the entry of communist "volunteers" into the Korean War, as a result of which the UN dubbed the PRC an aggressor. The United States and the KMT representatives therefore joined to win over a majority of states in the UN to oppose the replacement of the nationalist delegates.

After several years of unsuccessful attempts to gain entry, the PRC has taken a hostile line towards the UN, claiming that before it is seated, the UN must abrogate the 1951 resolution condemning the PRC as a Korean aggressor, and that the UN must "reform itself", by removing the "Chiang Kai-shek clique", and ceasing to be a tool of the big powers, a place where American and Soviet "imperialists" meet and try and enforce their demands on the rest of the world. The PRC claims that she has become a great power, armed with nuclear weapons, without the supposed benefits of UN membership, and the PRC consequently supported Indonesia's brief withdrawal from the world organisation, and has attempted to set up a counter-UN grouping.

Many countries would prefer to have the world's most populous state as a member of the UN. Some, such as the United Kingdom, consistently vote for the seating of the PRC, while asserting that this in no way implies that they wish to see Taiwan absorbed into the mainland. Many other states, however, are deterred from supporting the annual UN resolution calling for the seating of the PRC delegation, because they fear that if the resolution were approved, then the nationalist delegates would be forced to leave the UN.

The communists have never succeeded in getting a majority of UN members to vote for their representation. The closest they came was in 1965, when the vote was tied with 47 states voting for, and the same number against. As a general trend, support for the seating of the PRC has decreased, rather than increased over the years. In 1961, 48 states voted against entry, and 37 for (with 19 abstentions). The figures in 1968 were 58 against and 44 for (with 23 abstentions). Even if a majority were to vote for the resolution, this would not necessarily imply the seating of the communists (although it would give them a moral victory), because the question of Chinese representation is now considered by the UN General Assembly to be a substantive issue demanding a two-thirds majority. Here again, support for the view that it is a substantive issue has increased over the years, so that in 1968, 73 states favoured the two-thirds majority, and 47 opposed, with 5 abstentions.

One possible compromise, linked to a settlement of the Taiwan issue, would be a "two-Chinas" solution, whereby either the PRC would be admitted to the UN as a new member (Taiwan therefore retaining its seat on the Security Council), or Taiwan could be admitted as the new member, in which case the PRC would get the Security Council seat. However, both proposals are opposed by both sides, and also by the United States. Nevertheless, some solutions will inevitably be arrived at in the future, for most would agree that the People's Republic of China, whatever its form of government, has a role to play in the world community of nations.

SUGGESTIONS FOR FURTHER READING

An indispensable bibliographic aid for the study of Communist China is Peter Berton and Eugene Wu, Ed. Howard Koch, Jr., *Contemporary China: a Research Guide* (Stanford: The Hoover Institution on War, Revolution and Peace, 1967).

1: THE CHINESE REVOLUTION

For the early period of collaboration between the Nationalists and the Communists, see Xenia J. Eudin and Robert C. North, *Soviet Russia and the East, 1920–1927* (Stanford University Press, 1957). Also Harold R. Isaacs, *The Tragedy of the Chinese Revolution* (Stanford University Press, 1961). More details on the history of the CCP can be found in the following books: Conrad Brandt, Benjamin Schwartz and John K. Fairbank, *A Documentary History of Chinese Communism* (Harvard University Press, 1952); Jerome Ch'en, *Mao and the Chinese Revolution* (London: Oxford University Press, 1965); Robert C. North, *Moscow and Chinese Communists* (Stanford University Press, 1963); John E. Rue, *Mao Tse-tung in Opposition, 1927–1935* (Hoover Institution, Stanford University Press, 1966); Benjamin I. Schwartz, *Chinese Communism and the Rise of Mao* (Harvard University Press, 1964); Conrad Brandt, *Stalin's Failure in China, 1921–1927* (Harvard University Press, 1958); Richard C. Thornton, *The Comintern and the Chinese Communists, 1928–1931* (University of Washington Press, 1969); and Hsiao Tso-liang, *Power Relations within the Chinese Communist Movement, 1930–1934* (University of Washington Press, 1961). The official communist interpretation of their own history is in Ho Kan-chih, *A History of the Modern Chinese Revolution* (Peking: Foreign Languages Press, 1959), and Hu Chiao-mu, *Thirty Years of the Communist Party of China* (Peking: Foreign Languages Press, 1959). Also see the voluminous writings of Mao Tse-tung in his *Selected Works* (Peking: Foreign Languages Press, 1961–1965). For the period of war against the Japanese, see Edgar Snow's classic *Red Star over China* (New York: Grove Press, 1961) and Chalmers A. Johnson, *Peasant Nationalism and Com-*

munist Power (Stanford University Press, 1963). Also Boyd
Compton, *Mao's China: Party Reform Documents, 1942–44* (University of Washington Press, 1952); and Lyman P. Van Slyke,
*Enemies and Friends: The United Front in Chinese Communist
History* (Stanford University Press, 1967), as well as his book
*The Chinese Communist Movement: A Report of the United War
Department, July 1945* (Stanford University Press, 1968). More
detail on the Civil War and the events immediately prior to 1949
can be found in A. Doak Barnett, *China on the Eve of Communist
Takeover* (New York: Praeger, 1963); Lionel M. Chassin, *The
Communist Conquest of China* (London: Weidenfeld & Nicolson,
1966); Pichon P. Y. Loh, *The Kuomintang Débâcle of 1949*
(Boston: D. C. Heath & Co., 1965); Tang Tsou, *America's Failure in China* (University of Chicago Press, 1963); Herbert Feis,
The China Tangle: The American Effort in China from Pearl Harbor to the Marshall Mission (New York: Atheneum, 1965); Derk
Bodde, *Peking Diary: 1948–1949, a Year of Revolution* (New
York: Fawcett World Library, 1967); and John F. Melby, *The
Mandate of Heaven: Record of a Civil War, China 1945–49* (New
York: Doubleday Anchor Books, 1971).

2: THE CHINESE COMMUNIST PARTY

The nature of the "Thought of Mao Tse-tung" and Chinese communist ideology are analysed in Arthur A. Cohen, *The Communism of Mao Tse-tung* (University of Chicago Press, 1964), and
Stuart R. Schram, *The Political Thought of Mao Tse-tung* (New
York: Praeger, 1969). For the "debate" between Cohen and
Schram, see the symposium "What is Maoism?" in *Problems of
Communism*, vol. XV, no. 5 (September–October, 1966), and vol.
XVI, no. 2 (March–April, 1967). For a series of articles discussing
the origins of "Maoism", see those by Benjamin Schwartz and Karl
A. Wittfogel in *China Quarterly*, no. 1 (January–March, 1960),
no. 2 (April–June, 1960), and no. 4 (October–December, 1960).
The best full-length biography of Mao is Stuart Schram's *Mao Tse-tung* (Harmondsworth, Middx.: Penguin Books Ltd., 1967). Also
see Howard L. Boorman, "Mao Tse-tung: the Lacquered Image",
China Quarterly, no. 16 (November–December, 1963); Stuart R.
Schram, "Mao Tse-tung as a Charismatic Leader", *Asian Survey*,
vol. VII, no. 6 (June, 1967); and Benjamin I. Schwartz, "China
and the West in the 'Thought of Mao Tse-tung'," in Ping-ti Ho and
Tang Tsou (Eds.), *China in Crisis* (University of Chicago Press,
1968), vol. I, Book 1. See also the four volumes of Mao's *Selected
Works* published by Peking.

Information on the structure and functioning of the CCP can be located in A. Doak Barnett, *Cadres, Bureaucracy, and Political Power in Communist China* (Columbia University Press, 1967); Franz Schurmann, *Ideology and Organisation in Communist China* (University of California Press, 1968); James R. Townsend, *Political Participation in Communist China* (University of California Press, 1967); and also John W. Lewis, *Leadership in Communist China* (Cornell University Press, 1963). Translations of the 1956 CCP constitution can be found in Winberg Chai (Ed.), *Essential Works of Chinese Communism* (New York: Bantam Books, 1969), and John Wilson Lewis (Ed.), *Major Doctrines of Communist China* (New York: W. W. Norton & Co. Ltd., 1964). A translation of the 1969 Party constitution is in *Peking Review*, no. 18 (30 April, 1969). Additional information on the structure and functions of the CCP can be found in the following: Michel Oksenberg, "Local Leaders in Rural China, 1962–1965: Individual Attributes, Bureaucratic Positions, and Political Recruitment", in A. Doak Barnett (Ed.), *Chinese Communist Politics in Action* (University of Washington Press, 1969); John W. Lewis, "Leader, Commissar and Bureaucrat: The Chinese Political System in the Last Days of the Revolution", in Ping-ti Ho and Tang Tsou (Eds.), *China in Crisis* (University of Chicago Press, 1968), vol. I, Book 2; Donald W. Klein, "The 'Next Generation' of Chinese Communist Leaders," *China Quarterly*, no. 12 (October–December, 1962); Frederick C. Teiwes, *Provincial Party Personnel in Mainland China, 1956–1966* (New York: East Asian Institute, Columbia University, 1967); and Richard Baum and Frederick C. Teiwes, *Ssu-Ch'ing: The Socialist Education Movement of 1962–1966* (Berkeley: Center for Chinese Studies, University of California, 1967).

Major issues of the Cultural Revolution are discussed in A. Doak Barnett, *China After Mao* (Princeton University Press, 1967), and Jack Gray and Patrick Cavendish, *Chinese Communism in Crisis* (New York: Praeger, 1968). Also see Ralph C. Croizier (Ed.), *China's Cultural Legacy and Communism* (New York: Praeger, 1970). For documentary materials on the Cultural Revolution, see *The Great Cultural Revolution in China* (Hong Kong: Asia Research Centre, 1967), and K. H. Fan (Ed.), *The Chinese Cultural Revolution: Selected Documents* (New York: Grove Press, 1968). For a psycho-historical study, see Robert Jay Lifton, *Revolutionary Immortality: Mao Tse-tung and the Chinese Cultural Revolution* (New York: Random House, 1968).

There have been a large number of good articles written about the Cultural Revolution, its origin and development. A selection follows: Richard D. Baum, "Ideology Redivivus", *Problems of Communism*, vol. XVI, no. 3 (May–June, 1967), also his "China: Year of the Mangoes", *Asian Survey*, vol. IX, no. 1 (January, 1969); Philip Bridgham, "Mao's 'Cultural Revolution': Origin and Development", *China Quarterly*, no. 29 (January–March, 1967), and his "Mao's Cultural Revolution in 1967: The Struggle to Seize Power", *China Quarterly*, no. 34 (April–June, 1968); Parris Chang, "Mao's Great Purge: A Political Balance Sheet", *Problems of Communism*, vol. XVIII, no. 2 (March–April, 1969), also his "The Second Decade of Maoist Rule", *Problems of Communism*, vol. XVIII, no. 6 (November–December, 1969); David A. Charles, "The Dismissal of Marshall P'eng Teh-huai", *China Quarterly*, no. 8 (October–December, 1961); Lloyd Eastman, "Mao, Marx and the Future Society", *Problems of Communism*, vol. XVIII, no. 3 (May–June, 1969); Harry Gelman, "Mao and the Permanent Purge", *Problems of Communism*, vol. XV, no. 6 (November–December, 1966); John Israel, "The Red Guards in Historical Perspective: Continuity and Change in the Chinese Youth Movement", *China Quarterly*, no. 30 (April–June, 1967); Donald W. Klein, "The State Council and the Cultural Revolution", *China Quarterly*, no. 35 (July–September, 1968); L. La Dany, "Mao's China: The Decline of a Dynasty", *Foreign Affairs*, vol. 45, no. 4 (July, 1967); Roderick MacFarquhar, "Mao's Last Revolution", *Foreign Affairs*, vol. 45, no. 1 (October, 1966); Charles Neuhauser, "The Chinese Communist Party in the 1960s: Prelude to the Cultural Revolution", *China Quarterly*, no. 32 (October–December, 1967), and his article "The Impact of the Cultural Revolution on the CCP Machine", *Asian Survey*, vol. VIII, no. 6 (June, 1968); Franz Schurmann, "The Attack of the Cultural Revolution on Ideology and Organization", in Ping-ti Ho and Tang Tsou (Eds.), *China in Crisis* (University of Chicago Press, 1968), vol. I, Book 2; Benjamin Schwartz, "Modernization and the Maoist Vision: Some Reflections on Chinese Communist Goals", *China Quarterly*, no. 21 (January–March, 1965), and his article "The Reign of Virtue: Some Broad Perspectives on Leader and Party in the Cultural Revolution", *China Quarterly*, no. 35 (July–September, 1968); J. D. Simmonds, "P'eng Teh-huai: A Chronological Re-examination", *China Quarterly*, no. 37 (January–March, 1969); Tang Tsou, "The Cultural Revolution and the Chinese Political System", *China Quarterly*, no. 38 (April–June, 1969); C. K. Yang, "Cultural Revolution and Revisionism", in Ping-ti Ho and Tang Tsou (Eds.), *China in Crisis*, op. cit., vol. I, Book 2.

For biographies of many Chinese Communist leaders (and also prominent Nationalists), see the published volumes of Howard L.

Boorman's *Biographical Dictionary of Republican China* (Columbia University Press, 1966). Also see *Who's Who in Communist China,* two volumes (Hong Kong: Union Research Institute, 1969). A biography of Chou En-lai has been published by Kai-yu Hsu, entitled *Chou En-lai: China's Gray Eminence* (New York: Doubleday, 1968).

3: THE STATE STRUCTURE

Three excellent studies which give considerable coverage to the operation of governmental institutions are A. Doak Barnett, *Cadres, Bureaucracy and Political Power in Communist China* (Columbia University Press, 1967); Franz Schurmann, *Ideology and Organization in Communist China* (University of California Press, 1968); and James R. Townsend, *Political Participation in Communist China* (University of California Press, 1967). More details can be located in Ezra F. Vogel, *Canton under Communism: Programs and Politics in a Provincial Capital, 1949–1968* (Harvard University Press, 1969); Ying-mao Kau, "The Urban Bureaucratic Elite in Communist China: A Case Study of Wuhan, 1949–1965", in A. Doak Barnett (Ed.), *Chinese Communist Politics in Action* (University of Washington Press, 1969); Michel C. Oksenberg, "Aspects of Local Government and Politics in China: 1955–1958", *Journal of Development Studies,* vol. IV, no. 1 (October, 1967); and A. Doak Barnett, "Social Stratification and Aspects of Personnel Management in the Chinese Communist Bureaucracy", *China Quarterly,* no. 28 (October–December, 1966). Also see Barnett's book *Communist China: The Early Years, 1949–1955* (New York: Praeger, 1964).

The formal outline of the state structure of the PRC is in the *Constitution of the People's Republic of China* (Peking: Foreign Languages Press, 1961), which is reprinted in John W. Lewis, *Major Doctrines of Communist China* (New York: W. W. Norton & Co., 1964), and also in Theodore H. E. Chen, *The Chinese Communist Regime* (London: Pall Mall Press, 1967). For Mao's conception of the state form, see his "On New Democracy" (1940) in the *Selected Works,* vol. II; "On Coalition Government" (1945) in vol. III, and "On the People's Democratic Dictatorship" (1949) in vol. IV.

4: THE ORGANS OF CONTROL AND DEFENCE

A guide to communist legal literature is available in Tao-tai Hsia, *Guide to Selected Legal Sources of Mainland China* (Washington,

D.C.: Library of Congress, 1967). For further information on the legal system of communist China, see Jerome A. Cohen, *The Criminal Process in the People's Republic of China, 1949–1963* (Harvard University Press, 1968). Also Leng Shao-chuan, *Justice in Communist China* (Dobbs Ferry, New York: Oceana Publications, Inc., 1967). For article literature, see Ezra Vogel, "Voluntarism and Social Control", in Donald W. Treadgold (Ed.), *Soviet and Chinese Communism: Similarities and Differences* (University of Washington Press, 1967); Henry McAleavy, "People's Courts in Communist China", *American Journal of Comparative Law,* vol. II, no. 1 (Winter 1962); Allan Spitz, "Maoism and the People's Courts", *Asian Survey,* vol. IX, no. 4 (April, 1969); Sybille Van Der Sprenkel, "The Role of Law in a Changing Society", in Jack Gray (Ed.), *Modern China's Search for a Political Form* (London: Oxford University Press, 1969). For three articles on the procuracy, see those by George Ginsburgs and Arthur Stahnke in *China Quarterly,* no. 20 (October–December, 1964), no. 24 (October–December, 1965), and no. 34 (April–June, 1968).

Three excellent studies of the PLA are John Gittings, *The Role of the Chinese Army* (London: Oxford University Press, 1967); Alexander L. George, *The Chinese Communist Army in Action; The Korean War and its Aftermath* (Columbia University Press, 1967); and Samuel B. Griffith, *The Chinese People's Liberation Army* (New York: McGraw-Hill, 1967). Also see the *Selected Military Writings of Mao Tse-tung* (Peking: Foreign Languages Press, 1966). Other Western works include: Ellis Joffe, *Party and Army: Professionalism and Political Control in the Chinese Officer Corps, 1949–1964* (Harvard University Press, 1965); Richard M. Bueschel, *Communist Chinese Air Power* (New York: Praeger, 1968); and Michael Elliott-Bateman, *Defeat in the East: the Mark of Mao Tse-tung on War* (London: Oxford University Press, 1967). A good annotated bibliography of the PLA is Edward J. M. Rhoads, *The Chinese Red Army, 1927–1963* (East Asian Research Center, Harvard University, 1964). For article literature, see the special issue of *China Quarterly* devoted to Chinese military affairs, no. 18 (April–June, 1964). Also Samuel Griffith, "Communist China's Capacity to Make War", *Foreign Affairs,* vol. 43, no. 2 (January, 1965); Ralph L. Powell, "Commissars in the Economy: The 'Learn from the PLA' Movement in China", *Asian Survey,* vol. V, no. 3 (March, 1965), as well as his "The Increasing Power of Lin Piao and the Party Soldiers, 1959–1966", *China Quarterly,* no. 34 (April–June, 1968); and William Whitson, "The Field Army in Chinese Communist Military Politics", *China Quarterly,* no. 37 (January–March, 1969).

For an analysis of Maoist revolutionary strategy, see Samuel B. Griffith, *Peking and People's Wars* (London: Pall Mall Press, 1967), and also Ralph L. Powell, "Maoist Military Doctrines", *Asian Survey*, vol. VIII, no. 4 (April, 1968).

For studies of China's nuclear strategy, nuclear development, and arms control, see Morton H. Halperin, *China and the Bomb* (New York: Praeger, 1965); Alice Langley Hsieh, *Communist China's Strategy in the Nuclear Era* (Englewood Cliffs, N.J.: Prentice-Hall, 1962); Morton H. Halperin and Dwight H. Perkins, *Communist China and Arms Control* (New York: Praeger, 1965); Morton H. Halperin (Ed.), *Sino-Soviet Relations and Arms Control* (MIT Press, 1967). Also see Morton H. Halperin, "Chinese Attitudes Toward the Use and Control of Nuclear Weapons", in Ping-ti Ho and Tang Tsou (Eds.), *China in Crisis* (University of Chicago Press, 1968), volume II; and Ralph L. Powell, "China's Bomb: Exploitation and Reactions", *Foreign Affairs*, vol. 43, no. 4 (July, 1965).

5: ECONOMIC AND SOCIAL POLICIES

There are several good studies of the Chinese economy. See for example Cheng Chu-yuan, *Communist China's Economy 1949–1962* (New Jersey: Seton Hall University Press, 1963); Audrey Donnithorne, *China's Economic System* (London: Allen and Unwin, 1967); Alexander Eckstein, *Communist China's Economic Growth and Foreign Trade* (New York: McGraw-Hill, 1966); Li Choh-ming, *Economic Development of Communist China* (University of California Press, 1959); Nai-ruenn Chen and Walter Galenson, *The Chinese Economy under Communism* (Chicago: Aldine, 1969); Alexander Eckstein, Walter Galenson and Ta-chung Liu (Eds.), *Economic Trends in Communist China* (Chicago: Aldine, 1969); Alexander Eckstein, "Economic Fluctuations in Communist China's Domestic Development", in Ping-ti Ho and Tang Tsou, *China in Crisis* (University of Chicago Press, 1968), vol. I, Book 2; Dwight H. Perkins, *Agricultural Development in China, 1369–1968* (Chicago: Aldine, 1969); and Yuan-li Wu, *The Economy of Communist China* (New York: Praeger, 1965).

For details concerning the Great Leap Forward, see the translations of documents captured by the Nationalist Chinese during a raid on the mainland, in C. S. Chen (Ed.), *Rural People's Communes in Lien-Chiang* (Stanford: Hoover Institution Press, 1968). See also Isobel and David Crook, *The First Years of Yangi Commune* (London: Routledge and Kegan Paul, 1966); G. F. Hudson, A. V. Sherman, and A. Zauberman, *The Chinese Communes*

(London: Soviet Survey, 1959); and Henry J. Lethbridge, *China's Urban Communes* (Hong Kong: Dragonfly Books, 1961).

The problems that the CCP has faced with the intellectuals are dealt with in Theodore H. E. Chen, *Thought Reform of the Chinese Intellectuals* (Hong Kong University Press, 1960); Dennis J. Doolin, *Communist China: The Politics of Student Opposition* (Stanford: Hoover Institution on War, Revolution and Peace, 1964); Roderick MacFarquhar, *The Hundred Flowers Campaign and the Chinese Intellectuals* (New York: Praeger, 1960); Mu Fusheng, *The Wilting of the Hundred Flowers* (London: Heinemann, 1962); and Frederick T. C. Yu, *Mass Persuasion in Communist China* (New York: Praeger, 1964). A psychoanalytic interpretation of thought reform is offered by Robert J. Lifton, *Thought Reform and the Psychology of Totalism* (New York: W. W. Norton & Co., 1961). See also Merle Goldman, *Literary Dissent in Communist China* (Harvard University Press, 1967); and Richard H. Solomon, "One Party and 'One Hundred Schools': Leadership, Lethargy, or *Luan*?", *Current Scene,* vol. VII, nos. 19–20 (October 1, 1969).

For information on educational policy see Stewart Fraser, *Chinese Communist Education: Records of the First Decade* (Vanderbilt University Press, 1965); Hu Chang-tu, *Chinese Education under Communism* (Columbia University Press, 1962); and K. E. Priestley, *Education in China* (Hong Kong: Dragonfly Books, 1961). For details concerning marriage and the family, consult Helen Foster Snow, *Women in Modern China* (The Hague: Mouton, 1967), and C. K. Yang, *Chinese Communist Society: The Family and the Village* (MIT Press, 1959).

For an analysis of the CCP viewpoint on the national minorities, see George Moseley (Ed.), *The Party and the National Question in China* (MIT Press, 1966). Also see June Dreyer, "China's Minority Nationalities in the Cultural Revolution", *China Quarterly,* no. 35 (July–September, 1968); George Moseley, "China's Fresh Approach to the National Minority Question", *China Quarterly,* no. 24 (October–December, 1965), and his article "The Frontier Regions in China's Recent International Politics", in Jack Gray (Ed.), *Modern China's Search for a Political Form* (London: Oxford University Press, 1969).

6: FOREIGN POLICY

A good short text is Robert C. North's *The Foreign Relations of China* (Belmont, California: Dickenson Publishing Co., 1969). Other commentaries on Chinese foreign policy include: C. P.

Fitzgerald, *The Chinese View of Their Place in the World* (London: Oxford University Press, 1966); A. M. Halpern, *Policies Toward China: Views from Six Continents* (New York: McGraw-Hill, 1965); Richard Lowenthal, "Communist China's Foreign Policy", in Ping-ti Ho and Tang Tsou, *China in Crisis* (University of Chicago Press, 1968), volume II; Benjamin I. Schwartz, "The Maoist Image of World Order," in *Communism and China: Ideology in Flux* (Harvard University Press, 1968); and Tang Tsou and Morton H. Halperin, "Mao Tse-tung's Revolutionary Strategy and Peking's International Behaviour", *American Political Science Review*, vol. 59, no. 1 (March, 1965). For more detail, consult R. G. Boyd, *Communist China's Foreign Policy* (New York: Praeger, 1962); and Harold C. Hinton, *Communist China in World Politics* (Boston: Houghton Mifflin, 1966).

The development of the Sino-Soviet dispute has been written up by several competent analysts. See for example, Edward Crankshaw, *The New Cold War: Moscow v. Peking* (Harmondsworth, Middx.: Penguin Books, 1963); David Floyd, *Mao against Khrushchev* (New York: Praeger, 1963); William E. Griffith, *The Sino-Soviet Rift* (MIT Press, 1964); Klaus Mehnert, *Peking and Moscow* (London: Weidenfeld & Nicolson, 1963); Donald S. Zagoria, *The Sino-Soviet Conflict, 1956–1961* (New York: Atheneum, 1964). See also Zagoria's *Vietnam Triangle: Moscow-Peking-Hanoi* (New York: Western Publishing Co., 1967); P. J. Honey, *Communism in North Vietnam: Its Role in the Sino–Soviet Dispute* (MIT Press, 1964); Robert A. Rupen and Robert Farrell (Eds.), *Vietnam and the Sino–Soviet Dispute* (New York: Praeger, 1967); and William E. Griffith, *Albania and the Sino–Soviet Rift* (MIT Press, 1963).

For China's relations with Asian states, see A. Doak Barnett, *Communist China and Asia* (New York: Vintage Books, 1961); and Robert A. Scalapino (Ed.), *The Communist Revolution in Asia* (Englewood Cliffs, N.J.: Prentice-Hall, 1969). For policies towards some individual countries, also see Ruth T. McVey, "Indonesian Communism and China", in Ping-ti Ho and Tang Tsou (Eds.), *China in Crisis,* op. cit., vol. II; Sheldon W. Simon, *The Broken Triangle: Peking, Djarkarta and the PKI* (Baltimore, Md.: Johns Hopkins Press, 1969); D. P. Mozingo and T. W. Robinson, *Lin Piao on "People's War": China Takes a Second Look at Vietnam* (Santa Monica, Calif.: Rand Corporation, 1965); George N. Patterson, *Peking Versus Delhi* (London: Faber and Faber, 1963). On the question of the Overseas Chinese, see C. P. Fitzgerald, *The Third China* (London: Angus and Robertson Ltd.,

1965); Lois Mitchison, *The Overseas Chinese* (London: The Bodley Head, 1961); Gehan Wijeye-wardene (Ed.), *Leadership and Authority: A Symposium* (Singapore: University of Malaya Press, 1968); and Lea E. Williams, *The Future of the Overseas Chinese in Southeast Asia* (New York: McGraw-Hill, 1966).

A good article on Peking's relations with Latin America is Ernst Halperin, "Peking and the Latin American Communists", *China Quarterly,* no. 29 (January–March, 1967). For China and Africa, see the article by Richard Lowenthal in Z. Brzezinski (Ed.), *Africa and the Communist World* (Stanford: Hoover Institution, 1963); Emmanuel J. Hevi, *The Dragon's Embrace: The Chinese Communists & Africa* (London: Pall Mall Press, 1967); and George T. Yu, "Dragon in the Bush: Peking's Presence in Africa", *Asian Survey,* vol. VIII, no. 12 (December, 1968).

For the ramifications of US–China relations, see the following: A. Doak Barnett and Edwin O. Reischauer (Eds.), *The United States and China: The Next Decade* (New York: Praeger, 1970); Robert Blum, *The United States and China in World Affairs* (New York: McGraw-Hill, 1966); John K. Fairbank, *The United States and China* (New York: The Viking Press, 1962); and also his book *China: The People's Middle Kingdom and the USA* (Belknap Press of Harvard University Press, 1967); Fred Greene, *US Policy and the Security of Asia* (New York: McGraw-Hill, 1968); Robert P. Newman, *Recognition of Communist China?: A Study in Argument* (New York: Macmillan, 1961); A. T. Steele, *The American People and China* (New York: McGraw-Hill, 1966); Tang Tsou, *America's Failure in China, 1941–1950* (University of Chicago Press, 1963); Kenneth T. Young, *Negotiating with the Chinese Communists: the United States Experience, 1953–1967* (New York: McGraw-Hill, 1968); Hans J. Morgenthau, "The United States and China", in Ping-ti Ho and Tang Tsou (Eds.), *China in Crisis,* op. cit., vol. II; Lucian W. Pye, "China in Context", *Foreign Affairs,* vol. 45, no. 2 (January, 1967); Benjamin I. Schwartz, "Chinese Visions and American Policies", in *Communism and China: Ideology in Flux,* op. cit.; Richard H. Solomon, "Parochialism and Paradox in Sino-American Relations", *Asian Survey,* vol. VII, no. 12 (December, 1967). On the US involvement in Korea, see Glenn D. Paige, *The Korean Decision* (New York: The Free Press, 1968); and Allen S. Whiting, *China Crosses the Yalu: The Decision to Enter the Korean War* (New York: Macmillan, 1960). Concerning the complex of inter-relationships between the United States, Communist China, Taiwan and the United Nations, see Lung-chu Chen and Harold D. Lasswell, *Formosa, China and the*

United Nations: Formosa in the World Community (New York: St. Martin's Press, 1967); O. Edmund Clubb and Eustace Seligman, *The International Position of Communist China* (Dobbs Ferry, N.Y.: Oceana Publications Inc., 1965); and Robert A. Scalapino, "The Question of 'Two Chinas'", in Ping-ti Ho and Tang Tsou (Eds.), *China in Crisis,* op. cit., vol. II.

On relations between Britain and China, see Evan Luard, *Britain and China* (London: Chatto and Windus, 1962); and Brian E. Porter, *Britain and the Rise of Communist China: a Study of British Attitudes, 1945–1954* (London: Oxford University Press, 1967).

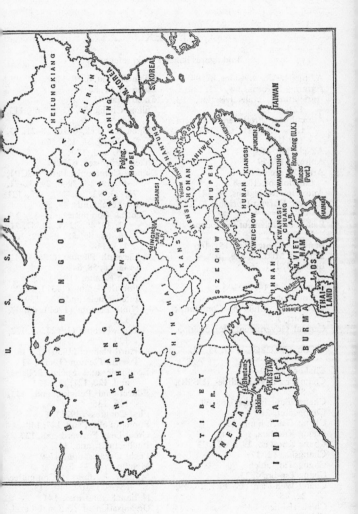

INDEX

Bold figures indicate main references